Young King Arthur in Brooklyn

rthur opened his eyes. There was a strange object by his face. It was large, brown and egg-shaped. He didn't have any idea what it was. Then he realized that he didn't have any idea where he was. Arthur raised his head, then turned over and tried to sit up. His head throbbed and he held it with both hands. "Oh, my head. What happened?"

"I think he's okay," Casey announced.

The air smelled strange, he realized. The conflagration of dense odors invading Arthur's nose told him that he was far from home. He made a sour, disgusted face. Arthur inhaled, trying to qualify his impressions while searching for the familiar scent of the forest he knew.

Then Arthur remembered the Duke. "Merlin, what happened?" He looked around. There was no castle and no forest, only a small brick structure nestled among some bushes not far away. But he was in a huge clearing completely surrounded by enormous trees. "Where am I?"

Young King Arthur in Brooklyn

David M. Korn

Jester  Books

Library of Congress Registration TXU 1-047-658
ISBN 0-9723382-0-9

All Inquiries
Jester Books
39 East 12th Street
#506
NYC 10003

Cover Illustration by Michael Houston

Produced at The Print Center, Inc. 225 Varick St.,
New York, NY 10014, a non-profit facility for liter-
ary and arts-related publications. (212) 206-8465

Manufactured in the United States
10 9 8 7 6 5 4 3 2 1

First Edition

To Susan

I

group of young boys ran through the center of the small village. They were dirty and loud, mean and reckless. They yelled at one another and everyone in sight. They scared old people and threw rocks at everything. They tormented young girls and shouted insults at their mothers. They taunted and threatened old men, then scattered like flies when challenged by passing knights.

They were an unruly mob, yet they had a leader, a boy named Arthur. Though it was barely apparent, he was more alert than the others and displayed more sense. They seemed to look to him. Maybe he was just a bit louder and quicker than the others, or faster and more impatient. They followed his lead. They were out to have as much fun in as little time as possible, for they had almost no span of attention. Sadly, there was little else for them to do but get into trouble, and it was the one thing they did well and without restraint.

It mattered little what they did or how they behaved, for they lived in a horrible place at an awful time. Life was short, and most people spent it cold, hungry, scared, poor and tired, or a combination of the lot. There was almost no trust, and even less hope. In fact, life was hardly worth living. But since it was all they had, they didn't really think about it, and some even managed a fair amount of enthusiasm for one thing or another.

There was, throughout their land, an abundance of violence and death. These were such regular daily occurrences that few actually noticed them. Indeed, mayhem gave a certain shape to the daily routine. Violence and death were among the small number of things that actually made sense to everyone. This was medieval England, backward and chaotic, hardly that place of romantic innocence that history fondly recalls.

Although there was a king, who was served by knights and a gentry, England was always on the verge of being torn apart by wealthy and powerful competitors, while the poor and superstitious simply prayed to be spared for just one more day. In fact, the country barely resembled a nation. There was nothing for anyone to believe in or be proud of, nor did its people even have a sense of their own identity.

Young Arthur was aware of none of this as he and his unruly friends left a path of destruction from one end of the village to the other. The village had no name, but the area was known by its huge surrounding forest, which belonged to the nearest lord. This fact, too, was of no interest to Arthur.

He could barely think beyond the next few seconds and gave no time at all to such weighty matters.

Arthur was about fourteen. His face and neck were dirty and his hair was long and messy. His clothes, which consisted of a course burlap tunic tied with an old rope at the waist, similar leggings ending in hard leather soles lashed to his feet, were makeshift, filthy and full of holes. These garments were the only things he wore and he rarely washed them and almost never took them off. But no one was accustomed to dressing much better among the peasantry. They were lucky to be wearing anything at all. If not for Arthur's intense, piercing blue eyes, he would have been unremarkable.

But when he stopped long enough to examine an object with his full attention, his gaze shone out from his grim countenance with the power of a lightening bolt. It was then that he appeared different from everyone else. These moments were, as yet, few and far between, but Arthur revealed an unmistakable awareness in them. One might even call it intelligence.

He now ran with a pointy stick in his hand. When he wasn't poking his friends or slashing at passing trees, he was thrusting it forward like a sharp sword, a danger to everything and everyone who got in his way. As he led his mates farther away from the village and into the forest, he seemed to get bolder and more reckless. He wanted excitement, he wanted adventure, he wanted a challenge. But most of all he just wanted to stab something, always an immediate source of good fun.

"Let's go down to the lake and try for fish!" one of the boys cried.

"No, 'tis too cold," said Arthur, deciding for all of them.

"What, then?" asked another.

"Let's see who can climb the tallest tree," offered a third.

"Again?"

"This day is not half over and already we are starved for activity."

"Yes, I fear the village is too small for our amusement."

"Let's visit the old man," said Arthur finally. There was no quick response to this suggestion, for it gave them all pause.

Arthur looked at the faces around him and took note of the fear in them.

The old man lived in a cottage far beyond the village in the densest part of the forest. All children were afraid of him and none had yet ventured to his door. They had only watched it from afar to see if he would emerge. Only a few had seen him, and when he stopped and bade them to show themselves they always ran away.

"What say you, then? We can be the first to knock upon his door."

"'Tis your idea, Arthur. You should be the first."

"Yes, you."

"Yes, yes," the rest of them repeated with increasing enthusiasm, each thinking that they would all hide out as Arthur went forth to live up to his word.

Arthur nodded. He knew that he could not refuse his own challenge. "Yes, then I will be the first," he stated for all to hear, including himself.

The small mob walked at a swift pace, summoning what courage they had to meet this unexpected challenge. The other boys watched Arthur's face as they went, waiting to see if he might appear to regret the suggestion and back down. Then, when he did not, and they found themselves in sight of the cottage, they thought they might all regret it instead.

Arthur stopped and lowered his stick.

"There it is," one of them whispered. They watched the small wooden shack from behind a clump of thick oak trees, securely out of sight. Now the immensity of the task was upon them, and the depth of their enthusiasm was tested.

"Maybe he's at not home," said one of them meekly.

But smoke was coming from the chimney so there was no such possibility. Where else would a scary old man be at such a time but away from the world deep in his secluded shack? "He is there and I shall know him come the end of this day," said Arthur boldly. But he could not encourage himself and had to secretly admit that he was, indeed, scared.

Arthur started forward, walking cautiously but without hesitation. He was determined not to stop until he reached the wooden front door. The cottage was better appointed than most in the region, and the grounds around it well-tended. The shutters were slightly open, but the inside was dim and

Arthur couldn't see anything through the windows. When he got within ten feet of the door he could plainly hear noises from inside. There were slight scrapings and odd tinklings, and the occasional mutter of an old man's craggy voice.

It was this that finally gave Arthur pause. He stopped and wondered if he should peek in through the window to get a look at the old man before he knocked on the door. If he knew what the old man looked like before he saw him, then perhaps it would be easier to stand his ground and not appear frightened. He realized for the first time that he couldn't just knock on the door and then run away. Arthur would have to enter the cottage and talk to the old man for this escapade to be successful.

Arthur walked the last few steps up to the door and got ready to knock. As he raised his fist he glanced over his shoulder to check on his audience. His friends watched in frozen anticipation, their mouths open as if expecting the worst. They were peering out from behind the trees, and seemed extremely far away, much farther than the distance Arthur had walked to the door.

Indeed, they were too far away for Arthur to read the shock in their faces, for the door had started to open before Arthur even turned back around. His fist was still raised and he was about to knock, when he found himself covered with a bucket of mysterious black water thrown from the open doorway. His friends were scared out of their wits and ran off in every direction. But they weren't quite sure what they'd actually seen.

"Aahhh!" Arthur cried. "What mess is this?!" The water was cold and acrid and his head and chest were as soaked as if he'd fallen in the lake.

"What are you doing in my doorway, boy? You're in the way."

"How was I to know you were going to throw open the door and drown me?" Arthur waved his hands and sprayed water back onto the old man.

"Don't do that you wretch, you're getting me wet!"

"You should throw your bog water out the back, not the front!"

"T'wasn't what you think, young man. Now come inside and dry yourself off. You'll catch your death out there in the autumn cold." Arthur entered the cottage and the old man closed the door firmly. Arthur forgot his apprehension and even his notions of adventure in this sudden turn of events. His expectations now ran only as far as the nearest dry rag with which to wipe himself off. He hardly realized that he'd effortlessly achieved his goal and was now the first, not only to see the old man close up, but also to talk to him and gain entrance to his cottage.

The old man handed Arthur a rag and proceeded to look him over. "What's your name, boy?"

"Arthur," he muttered.

"Arthur," the old man repeated curiously. "Arthur." He nodded as if the name meant something. "My name is Merlin."

Arthur stopped wiping his hands and tossed

the wet rag in the direction of a nearby table. He wrinkled his nose and smelled his hands, and then made a sour face. "I smell as if I might rot away right here. What was that you doused me with?"

"There's nothing to worry about. T'was only a potion I was working on."

"A potion?"

"Yes, a magical concoction. I'm a wizard, you see." Merlin spread his arms to indicate the surroundings, which Arthur had not yet noticed.

He looked around the small room and saw that it was indeed filled to overflowing with a variety of mysterious old books and huge jars of strange items. A work table was crowded with small bowls and instruments, and there was an open book in the center.

"What does the potion do?" Arthur asked, wondering if he might wake up the next day to find himself turned into a frog.

"Nothing, I'm sorry to say. It was a complete failure."

"I thought you were a wizard."

"I am, but I'm only a novice. I'm just starting out and still developing my gifts."

"You mean you don't know how to be a wizard yet?" Arthur exclaimed.

"It takes a long time, many years. You just don't snap your fingers and become a wizard." Merlin spoke with a disgruntled frown, which remained on his face as he looked down at the boy.

"Maybe you should just ply another trade," Arthur suggested faithlessly.

Now Merlin really became annoyed. His work

was difficult enough without the casual insolence of some unknowing whelp. "You know nothing of the world, little one. A wizard is a wizard and that is what he must be. It is the most honorable and carefully chosen vocation there is, and it can't be ignored or questioned. I'm as much a wizard as you are a mischievous youth, and we must both gladly accept our lot."

"Then how long's it going to take?"

"What?"

"To figure out what you're doing. What can you do now?"

"You try my patience boy. What are you doing here in the first place?"

Arthur was unprepared for this question. He hadn't been sure what he was going to say to the old man when he opened the door. Now that Arthur was inside the cottage and actually talking to him, not having a reason to have come seemed peculiar and ridiculous. Besides, he wanted to stay and keep talking to Merlin. He'd never met a wizard, not even a bad one, and it was the most interesting thing ever to happen to him.

"Well?" Merlin looked at him squarely and waited for an answer.

"Um, I was playing with my friends and they ran off. I set out to look for them... and got lost." Arthur was stunned by how good this sounded, and almost believed it himself. He was also impressed with his quick thinking, and felt a rush of satisfaction.

Merlin smirked, nodding suspiciously. "Hm, I see. Don't think I'm unaware of you children sneaking around outside, throwing rocks at my door and such. But maybe if you tell them all that I'm much less interesting close up, they'll go away and leave me alone."

Arthur wasn't sure if this meant he was about to be thrown out, but he sensed that he could now come back and engage Merlin again. If nothing else, it would give him something to do that was new and different. "So what can you do?" Arthur began to wander around, picking things up and looking at them closely.

"What are you doing? Don't touch that." Merlin was nearly on top of him, trying keep him away from everything. But the room was so small and there was so much in it, that it was all he could do to avoid disturbing things and knocking them over. When Arthur started to turn the pages in the book on the work table, Merlin decided that he'd had enough. "Now stop right there," he said emphatically. "I'll answer your questions if you just stay still and don't touch anything."

Reluctantly, Arthur complied. "Agreed."

"Good." Merlin reached past Arthur to return the book to the correct page. When Merlin took his hand away, he happened to brush Arthur's own hand and there was a flash. Merlin was stunned for a few moments, and lost all sense of where he was.

"What is it?" Arthur demanded.

"I've just had premonition."

"What's that?"

"A vision of the future."

"Are you sure?"

"Of course! I know a premonition when I see one. It's one of the things that makes me a wizard." He put his hand to his forehead. "This was a particularly strong one, very clear and intense."

Arthur became more interested. "What does it mean?"

"Well, I don't know exactly."

Arthur made a sour face. "I thought you said it was strong and clear."

"It was. That doesn't mean I understand it"

"Boy, what a lot of rubbish! What good is having a vision if you don't know what it means?"

"Once again, you display your boundless ignorance. These things are extremely complex. They can be interpreted in many ways. It's very important to not jump to any rash conclusions."

Arthur didn't appear persuaded.

"The truth and meaning become apparent in time. And as I develop my abilities, my visions will be sharper and I'll know what they mean immediately."

"What was the vision of?" Arthur asked. "Just what did you see?"

"I saw you," Merlin claimed.

"Really?!"

"Yes. You looked much different than you do now, but it was most definitely you."

Arthur didn't know what to say. It was the strangest thing, to be the subject of some wizard's premonition. He wanted desperately to know what it meant, at least for good or ill. For the first time in his short life, Arthur was forced to think of himself critically.

"You have to tell me what it means as soon as you know," he pleaded.

"By the time I know, young Arthur, you will know too. For the vision will have come true in some way."

"Have you ever had a vision of me before?"

"No, this was probably the first. But I've had many strange and obscure premonitions. And who knows, one or two might have been about you in some way."

"Then you can also have more!" Arthur exclaimed.

Merlin nodded. "That is also true. But we won't know until I have one. Now you must go home so I can go back to my work. But you may come visit me again, whenever you wish."

2

t was true that Merlin had had many
visions. It was also true that he'd had no
idea what any of them meant until they
came true. He'd tried many times to
interpret them, but he was always wrong. Despite
his explanation to Arthur, he'd become quite frustrated by his inability to understand what he saw.
Now, he tried to be more accepting of this process,
for he knew that it would take time to develop this
ability completely. But, like Arthur, he still wanted and expected to know the meaning of every
vision at once. They were the only things that
made him seem like a genuine wizard, and he
needed to master them before he could make his
mark in the world. A wizard who couldn't take
control of his visions was an embarrassment and a
laughingstock, like a knight who couldn't stay on
his horse.

Merlin couldn't help himself from making what
he considered a reasonable guess at the ultimate

significance of a premonition. It seemed to be part
of his learning process, and most of all, it made
him feel better. But, invariably, when the true
meaning was revealed, he would be as surprised as
anyone. His reaction would be stunned amazement, followed by reluctant acceptance, and finally, the thoughtful exclamation, "Yes, now I see the
sense of it!"

Merlin would then gratify himself by forgetting
just how wrong he'd been, and yield to the greater
and better revelation of the truth as if it exonerat-
ed his previous failure. It made him feel as though
he was making progress, and that was what he
cared about most. He refused to accept the years,
and possibly decades, that might pass before he
was a fully able, expert wizard with the magic of
the ages at his fingertips.

Also, Merlin wasn't even that old. To Arthur
and his friends he was an old man because children think all adults are old, be they thirty-five or
seventy-five. Merlin looked like a middle-aged man,
with just enough gray around his temples to make
him appear distinguished. But for a wizard he was
little more than a teenager, and as much of an adolescent as young Arthur. He had plenty of enthusiasm and anticipation, but little confidence of
success. His ability ran only to the simplest, most
benign tricks. Merlin couldn't turn animals into
anything, nor could he turn himself or anyone else
into any animals. He couldn't transport himself
anywhere, or summon any of the powers of nature,
except for an occasional bit of fire. When it came

to the Book of Potions, Merlin was as lost as a bad chef with a French cookbook. No matter how simple the recipe and how closely he followed the instructions, his concoctions still came out wrong. He wasn't even wise or knowledgeable about the ways of the world.

If not for the occasional premonition, Merlin was no more a wizard than any traveling fortune teller or superstitious old woman. But he now had some cause for hope, for his vision of Arthur was his strongest yet. And when he went to bed that night, his dreams were overwhelmed by more visions of young Arthur. But these also contained images from many previous visions throughout his life. He had strange and potent visions of Arthur, some as clear and real as if Merlin were watching them take place right before his eyes in the broad light of day. He saw Arthur as a knight, his armor shiny and immaculate. He saw Arthur sitting in a large chair with a confident expression on his face. He saw Arthur waving a gleaming sword in battle. He saw Arthur with other knights sitting at a big table. He saw Arthur confronting the ramparts of a huge, dark castle. He saw Arthur standing by a great piece of stone with something sticking out of it. It was as if Arthur had been added to all that Merlin had already seen, making sense out of it. The presence and significance of Arthur was so strong when Merlin awoke, that he realized every vision he'd ever had was about Arthur. Merlin had been having premonitions of the boy all along!

Merlin was now determined to see Arthur again

as soon as possible. He wanted to waste no time in seeing just what Arthur meant to his wizardry. If both his and the boy's destinies were indeed bound together, he reasoned, then they had to be together as much as possible for their futures to be fully realized. Merlin was so weary of fumbling around in his cottage, waiting to figure out the mysterious ways of magic, that he wasn't about to hesitate to throw his fortune in with the wild and impulsive young Arthur.

3

rthur went to visit Merlin the very next day, by himself. He had told his friends about Merlin, but never mentioned the vision. He didn't want them to think there was anything special or interesting about Merlin, so they wouldn't be curious to come to the cottage. Arthur even declined to tell them that he was a wizard, for he wanted Merlin all to himself. He didn't know what the premonition meant or what he expected from Merlin, but it had to be a lot better than running around poking things with sticks.

Arthur walked swiftly to the door of the small cottage. He knocked and then said loudly, "'Tis I Merlin, Arthur!" He wanted to make sure that Merlin knew he was out there, should he intend on disposing of another bucket of foul potion.

"Do come in, boy!" Merlin announced enthusiastically from inside.

Arthur thrust open the door eagerly and

stepped inside. Merlin was hunched over his work table, giving Arthur the impression that his life was a tireless pursuit of the inexplicable principles of magic and wizardry. "What're you doing?" Arthur queried, trying to see over the old man's shoulder.

"I'm eating my lunch."

"Oh, did you conjure it up out of thin air?"

"No, 'tis just a bit of leftover soup and bread."

"Did you have anymore visions of me?" Arthur asked hopefully.

"Not exactly. But I had a very important revelation instead. I realized that you have been the sole subject of my premonitions for many years."

Arthur was astounded. "I?! Really?!"

"Yes, there can be no mistake. Or at least not much of one."

Arthur looked the old man right in the face, wide-eyed and excited. "Why, what do they mean?"

"Ah well, that's always the fateful question, isn't it?"

"And... ?"

"I really couldn't say. But, mark my words, they mean something if anything means anything. We shall just have to wait and see."

"Maybe if you touch my hand again something else will happen and you'll know the answer." Without waiting for a response, Arthur grabbed Merlin's right hand and stood there, frozen in mute anticipation. "Well?!" he cried eagerly after a few moments.

Merlin shook his head casually. "Nothing." He waved Arthur away. "Such behavior is futile. One cannot just manipulate the ways of nature like that. The relevance of these visions will reveal itself in its own good time, and not before, no matter how much it might please us."

"So what do we do then? Just sit around and wait?"

Merlin said something incomprehensible. Arthur thought it was a magic chant, but then realized he was just mumbling through his soup. After he swallowed and cleared his throat, he said mysteriously, "Fate cannot be tempted, boy. But it can certainly be courted."

"You sure say things in a funny, roundabout way, Merlin. I've no idea what you mean."

"I mean that you and I will spend our days together. I will teach you the ways of the world, and by the time you are a mature and educated young man, we will know what fate has in store for the both of us."

"That sounds like little fun and a lot of work. What if nothing happens when we're done?"

"Nothing ever happens, I promise you that."

Arthur frowned. Now Merlin really wasn't making any sense.

"What?"

"What I mean is, something always happens because nothing is... Wait, let me start again. There's never just nothing, for something is always bound to happen. Understand?"

"I guess so. As long as something happens before too long and we know we're not just wasting our time."

Merlin smirked and looked him up and down. "What do you do with your days now, may I ask?"

"Oh well, whatever I want. I run about with my friends, swim in the lake when its warm. Play tricks on the knights and hide. Chase dogs and throw rocks at the girls in the village."

"I see."

"Climb trees and spit on people when they pass," Arthur continued. "Steal from the stalls at the marketplace. Make noises at the hangings and witch burnings. Just what boys everywhere do."

"And you're worried about wasting your time? No wonder the nation's in such a state."

"What did you do when you were my age?"

"I had my first premonition and was preparing myself to be a wizard."

Arthur nodded. "Then I guess we better get started. If we wait any longer you'll be too old and it'll be too late. Then I'll never know what all those visions mean."

"Don't worry, wizards live at least twice as long as other people. I've got plenty of time."

Arthur tugged at Merlin's arm. "But I don't. So let's go, start teaching me things."

"I assure you, the ways of the world will be yours. Now go outside and play and let me finish my lunch." Merlin turned back to his bowl of soup and resumed slurping away.

4

erlin and Arthur spent the first day of their new lives just walking through the forest around the cottage. Merlin proceeded to ask questions of Arthur, in order to find out just what he knew and how smart he was. Since there was no formal education for the peasants and boys worked from a young age, it was no surprise to Merlin that Arthur was bright and alert, but knew little about anything that was unrelated to mischief, petty theft and vandalism. Thanks to the occasional punishments by a local friar, Arthur had learned to read well enough. But he was starving for real knowledge and experience and was eager to learn and try new things.

Merlin decided that the best way to learn was by doing, so he bade young Arthur to challenge himself at every turn. He also realized that if they were going to make any real progress in their endeavor, they should confront the future as directly as possible. Since Merlin had a lifetime of

premonitions behind him, he knew that somewhere out there was a series of vital moments waiting to be uncovered. But why wait passively until
Arthur stumbled upon them, when he could just
as easily be steered towards them instead? This
seemed to Merlin what he was meant to do, use the
visions as a guide in the establishment of both his
and Arthur's true destiny. So they wasted no time
in what Merlin had called the courting of fate, an
undertaking blessed with the assurance of wisdom
itself.

One afternoon Arthur stood by the lake, looking
down at the water apprehensively. Merlin stood
behind him, hopefully peering over his shoulder. "I
don't see anything, Merlin."

Merlin was implacable. "Keep looking. In the
vision, you're astonished by something coming out
of the water."

"What?"

"I don't know. But it can't emerge from the
water unless it's down there in the first place."

"I've fished and swam in this lake all my life,"
Arthur protested. "And I never saw anything come
out of it but fish."

"Listen to me, boy. There was a bright light on
your face, as if you'd never seen something so...
so... bright!"

Arthur kept looking, but Merlin was still not
satisfied.

He stepped up behind him and began to push
him forward. "Maybe you're just too far away. Get
a little closer."

"I can see just fine," was the last thing Arthur said before he fell into the lake.

Merlin was still unconvinced. "Now that you're in there, swim to the bottom and feel around. It may just be hiding in the mud until the right time."

"Mflblsed," Arthur muttered in protest, his mouth full of fishy black lake water.

Arthur came up with nothing but a handful of slimy black mud, of little use even as a sign of things to come. It was most discouraging, especially to Merlin, who had expected results. He'd imagined a timely gathering of the instances of each vision, like the precise threading of a string of beads. Not that he'd counted on the instant success of getting everything at once, far from it. Merlin wanted to immerse himself in a substantial and challenging journey and relish its depth and complexity, which would be a better lesson for young Arthur. But there seemed to be so much to master and accomplish, and although he was nevertheless a wizard, who needed all the wisdom and experience of a thousand mortal men, he was also getting no younger.

"What now?" Arthur asked as he stood shivering in his dark wet clothes.

"We shall persevere," Merlin announced emphatically. "There are many more mountains to be climbed."

"I know of no mountains around here," said Arthur innocently, regarding the distant horizon.

"'Tis merely a figure of speech, Arthur. You must try not to think so literally."

"I assure you that I can't do that either. What are you saying this time, Merlin?"

Merlin sighed impatiently. "I mean there are more things for us to try. The source of at least one of these visions cannot be so impossible to uncover. There's no reason to conclude that we'll not know the meaning of one before too long. Then we'll finally be on our way, Arthur."

Merlin's enthusiasm was immediately infectious, and Arthur was eager to forge ahead. He was nearly dry again by the time they reached the site of the next premonition, a tall tree in the middle of the forest. "Now, up you go, Arthur," Merlin said without hesitation.

"Huh?"

"You must climb this tree to the very top."

Arthur stood at the base of the tree and looked up. It towered into the air as far as he could see, and the top was nowhere in sight. The trunk was so thick that a man twice the size of Arthur couldn't get his arms around it. "I don't know, Merlin. It looks too big. I can't even reach the first branch." He'd climbed more than his share of trees, but this one looked impossible. Even getting back down seemed like it would be no easier than going up.

"You were at the highest point in the kingdom, looking down on all Christendom with the assurance and authority of a king on his throne. That point must be this tree, which is the tallest in the whole forest."

"What for? It makes no sense."

"You mustn't doubt the righteousness of these

visions. They know you better than you know yourself. Far from being scared up there you seemed at home, as if you belonged there like any bird. Now no more hesitation. I'm sure that once you get to the top it will all make perfect sense."

It took Arthur more than a little while to get to the first branch, which he accomplished only after taking a running start and using Merlin's back as a ramp. But once there, the climb was not so difficult. The wind however, was a much different story, as was the unfriendly mother hawk who was sure that Arthur was after her young. Arthur only got about halfway up before her merciless attack. Fortunately, the thick branches broke Arthur's fall on the way down, and Merlin was there to prevent him from hitting the ground. The two of them lay in a heap at the base of the tree, Arthur suffering from extreme pain and Merlin from extreme disappointment.

They spent the rest of the day traveling from site to site and failure to failure. Arthur became increasingly doubtful of the whole endeavor, and Merlin more angry and frustrated. He'd expected to be heartily discussing their success over dinner and a warm fire, not going deeper into the forest more desperate and less hopeful than ever.

By the end of the day, Arthur had a half dozen other injuries to add to the first one. Among the various indignities, he was chased by an angry knight he tried to challenge, terrorized by a carpenter after sitting on every chair in his shop, and even beaten up by the father of a young maiden whom he said might be his one true love.

"Alas, this shall not come easy," Merlin admitted when they were on their way to the place of his final premonition.

"Maybe we should just wait until the visions come our way," Arthur said hopefully. He had little strength and enthusiasm left for these adventures. "I guess fate really shouldn't be tempted."

Merlin looked down at the boy and frowned with annoyance.

"Don't be too smart for thine own good. Despite our difficulties, these excursions have had the very ring of truth to them. A current of righteousness is unmistakable here and we'd be foolhardy to ignore it."

"Comforting words, Merlin. But I was better off when I had all my time to myself and no future. I've no patience for further pain and embarrassment."

"This routine is getting as old as Punch and Judy, Arthur. Now be quiet and spend the rest of the journey humbly contemplating the countryside." Arthur did as he was told, but far from considering the scenery, his mind could only wonder at what new indignity was awaiting him at the end of the trip. In any case, he vowed it would be his last, for he planned to free himself of Merlin's yoke at the next opportunity.

5

ere we are," Merlin declared at last. They came upon an enormous black castle very far from the village, at the distant edge of the forest. They'd walked for hours and the day was almost over. The sky was an ominous dark gray, nearly as dark as the castle itself. Together they thrust the surrounding lands into a foreboding mire unlike anywhere else in the region, as if this were the end of the earth and only the most dour and misguided of souls would dare live here. Even Arthur, most unafraid of the strange and unknown, found himself hesitant and dry in the throat when it came to summoning his youthful courage in the face of this confrontation.

"For the first time in our time together I question your judgement, Merlin. Surely we have no business in this awful place."

"You've questioned it every step of the way, boy! But now I sense common fear in your extensive words."

"Agreed, so I'm scared to death. What do you expect? I'm too young to enter the gates of hell. Let's go before we're ripped to shreds by a pack of merciless wolves. Besides, it's cold and I'm hungry."

"Enough whining. Mark my words, Arthur. This shall be your finest hour, for here is the very spot of my most portentous vision. 'Tis the black castle of the feared Duke of Flatbush."

"No!" Arthur cried in horror. "I've only heard of him in stories. I didn't even know he was real."

"As real as you and me, Arthur. But few have seen him and lived to tell the tale, for he is of a ferocious and merciless nature. He has no queen, no court, not even a single squire to keep him company."

Arthur listened with fascination, then looked up at the high and brooding castle walls with increasing awe. "Then he lives here all by himself. He must be mad."

Merlin shook his head slowly, and Arthur saw grave intent in his wise old eyes. "No, he's not alone. He has the company of just one, Melora, an ancient old witch who grants his every whim and cackles at his heartless jokes."

"You've heard him make jokes?!"

"Well, no, I haven't ever seen him or been inside his castle. But I imagine the two of them must have a good laugh every now and then to lighten things up. Now, we must gain access to his terrible domicile and duplicate the scene of my premonition."

Arthur nodded, having listened closely so he could extract the gist of Merlin's words amidst his unwieldy speech. "So we must get inside."

"Exactly!" Merlin declared.

Arthur looked at the door and spotted a huge iron knocker.

"Why not just knock like any visitor?"

"Ah yes, getting in is easy. Our concern is getting a proper audience with the Duke, rather than being quickly dispatched like bothersome peddlers."

"I see," Arthur agreed. "We can hardly tell him the truth and expect to be admitted."

"Let this be your first important lesson, Arthur. Unfortunately, deceit is the way of the world. Always conceal your true intentions and be prepared to lie until your goal is well in hand."

"I shall," said Arthur proudly.

"Now, here's what I propose," Merlin began, the glint of deception in his eye as he proceeded to explain his plan. When Merlin finished his lengthy explanation, Arthur approached the huge intimidating door of the castle and banged with the knocker three distinct times. There was no answer while Arthur waited, summoning his courage once again. It seemed that the most significant moments in his life were composed of waiting outside of closed doors.

"Maybe he's not there," Arthur whispered.

"Nonsense, he never leaves," Merlin said, standing right next to him. "Try again." Arthur did as commanded, but with an unmistakable timidity, as if he were afraid those inside might be asleep.

"Now what was that? You must knock with authority, as if you deserve to be admitted. Make them come running, and when they open the door you must step in with the urgency of one who is not used to being kept waiting. Like this." Merlin lifted the large iron ring and sent it crashing into the old wooden door as if it might smash it to splinters. The sound was thunderous, shattering the night all around them. Arthur covered his ears as Merlin continued to pound away. Arthur was growing increasingly worried, for if the Duke were as mean as reported, then surely this was no way to gain his favor. Such an introduction would only incur his wrath.

But upon Merlin's fifth pounding of the knocker, the huge door suddenly creaked ajar by itself. When Merlin let go of the ring and its echo died away, they were left with the open doorway and the cavernous entrance to the castle before them. Arthur and Merlin peered inside cautiously. They'd been ready to explain their presence to the Duke, and persuade him that they were not only worthy of access to the castle, but an invitation to stay the night and make themselves at home. They didn't know what to do now that they could just walk in unnoticed and unannounced and go anywhere they wanted with impunity.

"What now, Merlin? Should we go in?"

"I don't want to squander this one chance with an accidental violation of the Duke's domain. We can't very well stumble upon him somewhere deep in the castle and then try to convince him that we were just passing through and stopped to rest and get warm."

"But that's what you said our whole plan was to be."

"Yes, but I meant to tell him that when he met us at the door."

"Why don't we just say that nobody came to the door and when we realized it was open, we decided to come in." Merlin was uncomfortable exposing himself by actually having to tell the truth. "Okay," he managed to say. "But only because it's the only alternative to standing in front of this open doorway all night and still having no one know we're here."

So they walked in.

Their footsteps seemed especially loud in the cavernous silence of the anteroom of the castle. It was dark except for a burning torch on each wall to the right and left. Arthur could almost hear his own breathing as he and Merlin padded across the cold barren floor.

"Just where are we going, Merlin?" Arthur whispered as quietly as he could.

"To find the brightest room in the castle. That was the site of the vision. I saw you bathed in an all-consuming light, looking at the Duke with the most glorious expression. Now since the interior of this castle is so hopelessly dark, the scene must have taken place in the room which gets the most light."

"But it's almost night. There won't be any sunlight now."

Merlin sighed. "I thought my reasons were

obvious. That's why we must stay the night. The light is brightest when the sun comes up. We have to be in that room first thing in the morning or we'll miss our chance. Shh."

Merlin stopped suddenly and put his hand out to still Arthur. They'd come to a huge stone staircase extending up into the darkness. It was the entrance to the inner reaches of the castle. Now there was no turning back. It was Merlin's intention to find the right room and secretly spend the night there, so when the Duke found them in the morning, the conditions would be identical to those of Merlin's most powerful premonition, the same one he'd experienced when he touched Arthur's hand that very first day in the cottage.

6

erlin and Arthur crept up the cold stone steps towards the dank inner reaches of the castle. They could barely see their way, for the light was so dim and the moist, clammy air actually hung in patches of fog.

"This is the worst place I've ever been, Merlin. I'd gladly fall off a hundred trees and into a hundred lakes if I never had to set foot in this tomb again."

"Don't worry, my boy. T'will all be worth it by tomorrow."

"Maybe this time I'll only have to suffer a quick death, an improvement to be sure."

"This relentless doubt is getting on my nerves, Arthur. Have I ever lied to you?"

"Well... "

"Shh, we've reached the top of the stairs. Now we must decide which way to go, but we must be quick and quiet."

"Okay." Arthur yawned. The long day and the

poor light was making him sleepy. Merlin told him
to remain silent and stay close behind him. He led
Arthur down a narrow hallway and then through a
series of arches to a small closed door.

"I think we've made it," Merlin whispered as he
reached for the handle.

"I feel funny, Merlin."

"You're just scared. Stay close." Merlin pushed
steadily on the door and felt it give.

"What's happening?"

As Merlin continued to open the door, he too felt
a bit peculiar. Then there was a flash of light and
both he and Arthur succumbed to a strange dizziness, followed by an all-consuming blackness in
which they no longer knew where they were or
what was happening.

"Get up," a deep voice said. "Get up."

Merlin and Arthur were crumpled in a heap on
the floor. Arthur had his arms covering his head.
He removed them slowly and opened his eyes.
Merlin stood up and rubbed his forehead. The first
thing Arthur saw was a gaunt but imposing man
dressed all in black standing in the corner of the
small dark room. His expression was mean, but
thoughtful as well.

"Merlin, where are we?"

"You're in my dungeon. Now what are you
doing here in my castle?"

"You must be the Duke," Merlin offered, almost
pleasantly.

"I am."

Merlin stepped forward to introduce himself.

"Well I'm—"

"I know who you are. What do you want?"

"You know us. How?"

"Melora informed me. Just as she informed me of your arrival before she brought you here." Standing near the Duke, somewhat hidden by the shadows, was a woman who looked at least a hundred-and-fifty years old. She opened her craggy mouth and out came a laugh so hideous and excruciating that Arthur had to turn away from her to withstand it.

"She brought us here? But why?"

"To keep you from wandering around the castle."

"We knocked, but no one answered."

"No one answered because no one was interested in seeing you. That was your invitation to go away."

"I thought the Duke of Flatbush just does away with people who cross his path. Turns them into frogs and slugs and—"

"Now why would I do that?" Melora laughed again, her whole ancient body rattling uncontrollably with the awful sound.

"To add to your reputation as a merciless tyrant."

The Duke sighed. "If I did that to everyone who darkened my door I would never have such a reputation, for there'd be no one to spread the word that I do away with everyone who crosses my path."

"Yes, I see the sense of it," Merlin exclaimed. "So you just do away with an occasional few then."

"No, I did away with just one, a long time ago. Everyone since then I've just scared and threatened so they'll add to the legend. I can think of no bigger waste of good magic than turning people into frogs and slugs every time they drop by." Melora laughed again, as painfully as ever.

"You were right Merlin, she does laugh at all his jokes."

"Actually, she laughs at everything I say," the Duke replied. "It's practically the only sound she ever makes."

"It's horrible. How can you stand it?"

"Oh I like it, because it's so hideous that it completely unnerves everyone. It's very effective. Now, before I command Melora to send you back where you came from in the blink of an eye, why have you come?"

"Ah, well," Merlin began, "that's rather complicated." He cleared his throat to establish his authority. "Tell me, which is the brightest room in the castle, in the morning that is?"

"Oh, for mercy's sake. Melora!"

The last thing they heard was that insufferable laugh, for true to his word the Duke sent them back into the forest in the blink of an eye. When the dizziness wore off and they looked up again, Merlin and Arthur were surrounded by the same trees they had passed on the way to the castle.

"Wow," Arthur cried. "She's got some power. I'll bet you wish you could do that."

Merlin frowned. "Envy is a mortal temptation," he said disdainfully. "Nevertheless, one cannot help but be impressed by her gifts, the unspeakable hag."

Arthur turned to look behind him. The castle stood in the distance as it had upon their approach. "What now, Merlin? You must have another plan."

"I think not. Shan't we call it a day."

"If only you could turn us into two birds. Then we could fly in the window of the room and the Duke would never know we were there."

"A fine idea, Arthur. Though I doubt even that entrance would pass Melora's notice."

"But there are no more visions to follow."

Merlin nodded. "Yes, we'll just have to be content to wait until fate shows us the way of its own accord."

"Really? Then there's nothing else to do?"

"Nothing."

Arthur nodded. He should have known. "'Tis just as well. I'm neither surprised nor disappointed, after all my pain and trouble. I was quite the fool for expecting to be rewarded so easily."

"I, too, I must admit. But then, maybe failure is the best teacher."

Arthur groaned and waved his hand in disgust. "I'm tired of learning the hard way. What good is success if it doesn't come readily?"

Merlin said nothing. For once, he had no quick answer to placate the boy.

Arthur hung his young head, and Merlin, his friend and mentor, hung a sympathetic hand on his small shoulder. They began the long trek back through the forest to the village, where Arthur lived with his father, Ector, and his older brother, Kay. Merlin, after this long and trying day, was looking forward to an equally rigorous period of introspection and re-dedication to the lifelong pursuit of the incomprehensible ways of magic and wizardry.

"What's that?" Arthur cried, pointing to a strange obstacle up ahead. They had gone only a short way, when they spotted the object far in the distance. Arthur had no idea what it was, but Merlin recognized it immediately. Suddenly, his face lost all its color.

"It can't be," he said, stopping slowly. "I think it is."

He crept closer, then completely lost his head and started running towards it as fast as he could. "It is! Oh I can't believe it! It is!" By the time Merlin reached the large object he was jumping up and down like a child on Christmas morning. "Arthur!" He turned and waved at him, still jumping up and down. "Arthur, come quick!"

Only when Arthur got to the huge object could he see what it was. He stood next to Merlin, whose face was still radiant with excitement, looking at a huge stone with a sword sticking out of it. It was the strangest thing Arthur had ever seen, especially since he was sure that it wasn't there before. The sword had been plunged deep into the stone, right up the hilt. As if he still couldn't quite believe his eyes, Merlin went up to it and took hold of the handle and tried to pull the sword out.

"It won't even budge," Merlin announced.

"Arthur, this is no ordinary sword in a stone."

"I don't understand. Who could've done this and what's it doing in our path?"

"No one, that's the point. No one could've stuck this sword into this piece of stone. It just appeared by itself."

"Why?"

"It's a sign," Merlin said, almost deliriously. "A real sign. This was in one of my visions. But I knew of no place where it might be. Little did I know that fate itself would provide for us. She waited until we'd arrived at the very end of our quest."

"I still don't know what it means."

"It's a symbol of a new era, one of unity and peace. It's a call to bury our weapons and let down our guard, be trusting and forthright. I see the sense of it so clearly now. It's a great day for the whole nation, Arthur."

Arthur scowled. "But what does it have to do with me?"

Merlin approached him and placed his hands on Arthur's thin shoulders. "Don't you see, my boy? You are the messenger! It's you who'll spread the word!"

Arthur looked at the golden handle of the sword. It seemed to say a lot for a piece of metal sticking out of hunk of rock in the middle of nowhere. "I don't know, Merlin."

"Now is not the time for humility. We've finally got what we've been desperate for, and we must be true to our destiny.

We'll tell everyone in the village, and then—"

"But what about all those other visions you told me about? The ones where I'm in armor, fighting in battle, leading great knights, and—"

Merlin threw up his hands and dismissed his protest completely. "A test, nothing more. You mustn't believe every vision you see. Forget all the others, for we shall be guided by this one alone!"

7

erlin and Arthur walked back to the village, confident in their new mission. Merlin told Arthur to get a good night's sleep, for tomorrow they would announce their discovery and disclose its meaning. Merlin went back to his cottage, eager for the night to end and the new day to begin. But he was too restless to sleep himself, and spent half the night poring over his sacred books and papers, searching for some secret indication of what was to come.

His initial excitement had obliterated all doubt and hesitation, but now he found himself beginning to get just a little curious about the immediate future. Was recognition and greatness finally upon him? he wondered. Was it all to be this easy?

Surely, he thought, I'm not yet worthy of such a glorious reward. The next day, word spread quickly of the strange stone in the middle of the forest. Arthur had told only a handful of people of the object, but rumors were all over the village before the sun was fully overhead. Unfortunately, the chatter got out of control almost immediately, for there were so few interesting occurrences in the village that the sword in the stone suddenly became the most discussed subject since the defeat of the Saxons.

The excitement reached a peak when everyone could no longer wait to see the thing. They all left their homes and shops and work places to venture into the forest in search of the stone. Even the knights and squires left their posts and quarters to join the throng. Merlin and Arthur were among the crowd, having gotten a late start when they realized what was happening around them. Merlin had hoped to get there ahead of everyone else, to preside over the event and make sure it went as planned. The sudden chaos now made him anxious. It was all happening too fast and no one around seemed to know who had made the discovery or what it meant. He even worried that fate would play a cruel joke on him and cause the stone to vanish completely.

But soon enough, the huge stone came into view again, and just as before, the shiny sword with the gilt handle was sticking out of it for all to see. For all their eagerness and excitement, everyone slowed down and became quiet when they neared the thing. Truly, they had never seen anything like it in their lives or imagined it in their dreams. When the crowd got as close to it as it dared, it came to a stop as all eyes fixed on the same spot, the gold handle of that amazing sword.

Men took off their hats and women folded their hands, but no one spoke a word. Even the usually brash and arrogant knights were stunned in their places.

The moment was precious, for it allowed Merlin to make his way to the head of the mob and get everyone's attention. He raised his hands and got ready to speak. Lost in the center of the crowd, Arthur watched with heart-pounding anticipation, as if he hadn't been there the day before and didn't already know what the sword in the stone meant.

"My friends, this is a great day for us all!" Merlin began rousingly.

"Who are you?!" someone called out.

"Merlin, the wizard."

"I never heard of you!"

"Me neither," said another, and was followed by a chorus of baffled agreements, shrugs and shakes of the head by others in the crowd.

"All right then, I'm a wizard! But in a thousand years I'll be known far and wide for this very moment you're all about to witness. The sword in the stone is a story that shall ring down through the ages and be hailed as one of the greatest legends of all time. It was discovered by myself and this young boy..." He searched the crowd for Arthur, but couldn't spot him. "Arthur, are you out there? Come up here, boy!" A brief murmuring passed through the throng. Then it parted as Arthur excitedly pushed his way to the front, where he eventually joined Merlin before the huge stone. Merlin put a hand proudly on his small shoulder. "This boy Arthur and I came upon the stone in the forest just yesterday, and we spread the word that brought you all here today!"

Merlin paused to give everyone in the crowd a few moments to reflect on his words. He imagined that they were all dying to be informed of the details of the event, and were ready to contain their excitement to listen to what he had to say next. There were whispers among the crowd, but no one seemed to glance at Merlin and Arthur in a way that indicated astonishment or gratitude. Merlin took this as a sign of the villagers' collective confusion, and proceeded to declare the meaning of the sword in the stone in no uncertain terms.

"You are all disturbed and confused by the appearance of this strange object! But fear not, for it is a sign of a new era of peace and trust!"

"What?! No it's not!"

"That's not what we were told!"

Now it was Merlin who was confused. "What? What were you told?!"

"That it's for the new King!"

"Yes, the King."

Merlin could see the nods and hear the words of enthusiastic agreement and he became even more perplexed. He couldn't imagine what they were talking about. "What about the King?" he asked with a sour expression, his hands firmly planted on his hips.

"Whoever pulls the sword out of the stone is the new King!" someone called out above the growing din.

Well this was the most ridiculous thing that Merlin had ever heard. He looked horrified. How did they ever get that idea? he wondered incomprehensibly. Fools, he thought. Stupid, backward fools! But he intended to set them straight immediately. He raised his arms again, this time in protest.

"Who told you that?!" Merlin demanded.

"That's just what I heard!"

"Yes, me too."

"And me!" That's what they all seemed just to have heard, as if no source was actually responsible for the news.

Merlin glanced down at Arthur critically. "Just what did you tell these people?"

"I told them what happened, how we found the stone and what it meant."

"Then where did this crazy notion of pulling the sword out and becoming King come from?" Arthur shrugged and said nothing.

Merlin looked out at the crowd and addressed them with authority.

"The sword has nothing to do with being King! It is a symbol of peace and unity! It's a great plea for us to put away our weapons once and for all!"

Disagreement overwhelmed the crowd, and threatened to turn into hostility. It was apparent to Merlin that everyone wasn't just misinformed, they didn't want to believe the truth about the sword in the stone. But Merlin was still sure that he could convince them otherwise.

"My friends, the symbol is obvious. The sword

is buried in the stone! It cannot be pulled out! But if any of you do not believe me, then by all means, step up here and try to pull it out! And if you can," Merlin laughed, "then you are surely and rightly the next King of England!" Merlin stood aside and motioned blithely to the stone behind him. He expected everyone to see the absurdity of the challenge and dismiss the entire notion, but he was not yet possessed of the keen perception that he would develop later in his long life.

Merlin and Arthur were almost trampled by the mad rush of knights, farmers, artisans and other men eager to pull the shiny sword from the huge stone. The spectacle of all of them yanking on the steadfast sword as hard as they could was astounding to even their fellow villagers. Merlin stood there in stunned silence, awed by their stupidity. Each screamed for the others to let go, not realizing that if fifty pairs of hands could make no difference, then neither could just one. It was a good thing that no one succeeded in freeing the sword, for the first thing he would most likely have done with it was start to slice up his competitors.

"Oh, for mercy's sake!" Merlin cried. "Now are you all convinced?! It hasn't budged so much as an inch!"

"I don't think they heard you," Arthur said, watching the futile contest continue unabated.

Merlin placed his hands on his hips and shook his head in disgust. "Why anyone would want to be king of such a lot of half-wits anyway is a complete mystery to me!"

"What shall we do, Merlin?"

"Nothing. When they realize that it just can't be removed they'll stop. Then they'll have no choice but to listen to reason."

"I hope you're right. But they don't look like they're going to give up very soon."

And they didn't give up. They continued to yank and pull and push on the sword. When some men took short rests, others jumped into the fray to take their places. Men rested two and three times, going back to try again and again. And when they weren't fighting the immovable sword, the men were fighting one another. Each seemed to think that his failure was the fault of the rest, and if they would all just get out of the way his triumph was assured.

Merlin and Arthur waited patiently until all the men had exhausted themselves and fallen aside in a huge heap. When the last few hopefuls, a small but enthusiastic group of young boys and old men, had finally tried their luck and given up, Merlin stepped forward to address the throng for the last time. When he stood upon the rock to emphasize his authority, he and Arthur were the only men present who still hadn't touched the sword in the stone that day.

"Happy now? You've all made complete fools of yourselves. But worst of all, you've displayed a terrible lack of faith. Fate has made its proclamation, and it's been profoundly ignored and challenged. You've turned a sacred day of peace into one of—"

"All right old man, you've made your point!" someone shouted.

"And made it and made it!" added another.

Merlin smirked in disgust. "The point is whether you all can humbly accept the great decree we've been fortunate enough to receive. Well?" Merlin waited for a response, his hands expectantly on his hips again.

There were assorted groans of acquiescence among the dejected crowd, but nothing that was the stuff of legend. Merlin was not satisfied.

"I don't hear you! This is hardly the way to begin a new era!" Merlin saw a kind of collective nod, accompanied by a grudging sound of acceptance that was pronounced enough to be taken for agreement, however reluctant. "There now, that's better," Merlin announced with encouragement. But he knew that this was just the beginning of a long journey. After a thousand years of violence, brutality and superstition, a new age of peace, trust and community would take some work, no matter how much faith there was or how many miracles fate provided.

The men slowly regained their strength and returned to their feet, and with the rest of the crowd straggled back towards the village.

Merlin was proud and satisfied. It was only afternoon, and already the first day of this new era was a smashing triumph. He was possessed of its infectious spirit and had a renewed sense of himself. His duty was now clear, to develop his great gifts and use them for the selfless benefit of his nation in the service of its new identity. Fate had been kind enough to use him for its messenger, and he was more grateful than ever. He was only too happy to pay her back by dedicating his life to the cherished art of magic and prophecy.

Merlin stepped down off the stone. "Let's go home, Arthur," he said over his shoulder, and proceeded humbly to follow his countrymen back through the forest.

"Coming, Merlin." Arthur started to take off after him, but something held him back after only a few steps. He turned and his gaze was drawn to the sword in the stone, now all by itself in the silent clearing. He hesitated for a moment, then stepped quietly onto the huge rock. One good pull, Arthur thought. Just for fun.

"Merlin, look!" Arthur shouted, jumping down off the stone and running after him. "Look, look!"

Merlin turned around and was stunned by the sight of Arthur with the big shiny sword in his grip. He put his hand to his forehead in horrified amazement. "Oh no! Where did you get that?!"

"I pulled it from the stone!" Arthur said as he came running up to him.

Merlin threw up his hands. "Now what am I going to tell everyone?"

"Just that I'm King of England!"

8

erlin considered ordering Arthur to put the sword back before anyone saw that it was free of the stone. But there was no stopping the boy now, for he ran past Merlin lugging the sword with both hands still screaming, "Look look, everybody! Look look!" Merlin could only shake his head and watch helplessly.

It would be wonderful to describe how all the people stopped and gazed in amazement at Arthur when he presented the sword to them, and how they rejoiced at his unlikely but inspiring triumph. But the truth is that they had little reaction at all. Someone pointed and shouted, "Look, he has the sword!" And another cried, "Yes, he's pulled it from the stone!" And a few people stopped and turned, their faces slack with genuine surprise. But the enthusiasm ended there, for the sight of young Arthur with his small dirty hands around the huge shiny sword was more baffling and disappointing than anything else. He was inexperienced and undeserving. How could that sword, which had resisted all the knights and strong young men in the crowd, be rightfully promised to no one but a mischievous and impulsive young boy? Even fate, no matter how mysterious, was no suitable explanation for such a destiny.

"But I'm King!" Arthur protested as the crowd, unmoved and uninterested, continued to walk back to the village. "I have the sword! I pulled it from the stone! You said it means I'm King! You can't change your mind now!" Red-faced with anger, Arthur turned to his mentor after they were alone in the forest again and said painfully, "But I'm King, Merlin. Why won't they listen?"

Merlin put his hands together and nodded sympathetically. "I know you are, my boy. 'Tis a surprising conclusion, in more ways than one can count."

"What shall we do?"

Merlin looked down at Arthur. Under the circumstances, the crowd's reaction wasn't that peculiar. The weapon was bigger than Arthur himself, and even made him look a bit smaller. Indeed, it made him look diminutive and ridiculous, like a child playing with his father's sword. He needed to hold it with both hands because he could barely lift it otherwise. Merlin hoped that Arthur would grow into it soon enough, or he wouldn't be taking the throne anytime soon.

"Apparently Arthur, fate is a mysterious and unpredictable mistress. We'll have to navigate our path to destiny with great care."

"But what shall we do to make everyone follow me? Either I'm King or I'm not," he pouted.

Merlin nodded thoughtfully. "Oh, you most certainly are. The question is what it will take to convince everyone of this undeniable fact."

"But how?" Arthur insisted petulantly.

"It seems to me," the old man said with a finger in the air, "that to be thought of as a king you then must act like a king. Do you take my meaning, Arthur?"

The boy nodded carefully. "I think so, Merlin."

"We shall soon see. Now, let's go straight to the village and prepare for your... coronation."

Merlin conducted Arthur through the village, where they stopped at the shops of various tradesmen to acquire royal accoutrements for the young king. By the time they finished, Arthur was fully outfitted in the splendor appropriate for any leader of the realm. Merlin was also quick to call him sire as frequently as possible, for the benefit of the dubious public. Merlin noted to Arthur that every detail of his transformation was vital, for only when he was treated like a king would he be followed as one. "Yes," Arthur said of his new title, "I see the sense of it."

When they finally got back to Merlin's cottage, no one could doubt that Arthur was the very picture of royalty. Along with his shiny sword, he now possessed a bright purple tunic, armor of chain mail for his arms, neck and head, now more neatly shorn, strong leather footwear and leggings, and a belt and sheath for the sword. He had trouble walking upright under the weight of it all, but

Merlin assured him that he would get used to it and the effect was worth it.

Merlin was correct, for the transformation was more than cosmetic. Although there were laughter and insults at first, Arthur had gained a new confidence by the time his outfit was complete. Looking like a king made him feel like a king. By the end of the day, Arthur was possessed of an assurance of purpose and bearing, as well as an arrogance beyond his years. Even what might be called righteousness.

As they drank cider in the cottage, Merlin looked Arthur over critically, as if for the first time as this new identity. "Well Arthur," he began, nodding proudly, "this must be the longest day of your life, for you seem to have grown up in the course of it."

"I sure feel different."

"And you are, my liege. Your very presence commands authority. You will not even have to inform anyone that you are King, for all will know the fact immediately. Surely everyone will kneel before you on sight."

Arthur liked the sound of this, and couldn't wait to walk among the villagers once again. He didn't know what he would do as King, but he knew for sure that he would love being King. It had to be much better than being just a pitiful adolescent to whom no one paid any attention, and didn't even regard as a real person.

They finished their cider and Merlin explained his strategy.

They would go directly to the local magistrate and demand an audience, then announce that Arthur was the new King of England, as proclaimed by the recent decree of the sword in the stone. It was Merlin's intention to make full use of the rumor mill this time. Since everyone already knew of Arthur's removal of the sword, they would immediately be prompted to accept Arthur as King once they learned of his official recognition. No one would question Arthur's right to the throne if he thought that everyone else had already accepted it. Word would soon spread of Arthur's royal status throughout the land, making his ascendancy a fait accompli.

This approach seemed unassailable to Arthur, and the next day they set off to the village, more confident and determined than ever. They passed through the village with regal pride, acting as only a king and his wizard were expected to act. There were whispers and eyes followed them, but with humility and deference. Merlin noted this and commented to Arthur under his breath. "You see Arthur, the difference is already apparent. The groundwork has been well-laid."

But when they got to the residence of the magistrate on the far side of the village, they were rebuffed with impunity. They gained an audience without question, but it was solely for the amusement of the magistrate and his officers. They had heard about the young boy, the old man, and the sword that came from the stone in the forest, and they were anxious to see the subjects of this hilarious and unbelievable masquerade. They were especially amused at the sight of Arthur in his regal splendor, and laughingly commented that he may not be taken as King, but he might have a most promising future as court jester. Merlin's eccentric protests only produced more laughter, and then the two upstarts were shown the door.

The story was the same in the parlors of every official in the area, no matter how lowly and inconsequential. Arthur's confidence, which had initially motivated him to be bold and demanding in the face of this resistance, deteriorated with each new visit. What had started out as outraged protests, eventually became nothing more than pathetic cries to be taken seriously. The fact that Arthur couldn't take three steps without tripping over the sword was also no help at all. By the end of the day, Arthur had been reduced to an anonymous adolescent once more. Far from his being proclaimed King and Merlin a great wizard, they'd become a laughingstock, and this was the word that spread throughout the land. When they finally traipsed back through the village at the end of the day, it was to the derisive laughter of every knight, tradesman, artisan and peasant in sight. Once again, idle chatter had done them in.

Merlin burned with a desire to turn them all into slugs squirming in the mud, but he just didn't have the power. Wizards were supposed to be above such frustrations, or the world would have perished by their wrath ages ago. But this was more than even a novice could stand. He was now more determined than ever to right this great injustice and see young Arthur on the throne.

"Maybe fate changed her mind, Merlin."

"Nonsense. The decrees of fate are carved in stone."

"But—"

"Fear not, Sire. You'll be King soon enough, for I have formulated a new plan."

"I can't wait to hear it," Arthur said dubiously.

"It seems that people only believe what they find convenient and easy. We must shake them out of their complacency. You must be outraged by this display of disrespect. A true king would not accept it."

"Meaning what?"

"A king without the support of knights is no king, Arthur. The truth is, we must force your ascendancy on the ignorant rabble as well as competing noblemen. And the best way to do this is by enlisting the alliance of the most feared lord in the kingdom."

Arthur was confused, then he realized what Merlin must be suggesting. "Oh no, you don't mean the—"

"That's right! The Duke of Flatbush!"

9

hat evening found Merlin and Arthur once again on the far side of the forest at the threshold of the Duke's castle. On the way, Merlin had done wonders in restoring Arthur's faith, both in himself and this new endeavor. He had convinced Arthur that if the Duke saw him in his regal splendor and accepted the boy's true destiny, he would realize the wisdom of making Arthur his ally. He'd explained away Arthur's fear that the Duke would have the same reaction as everybody else by stressing that the Duke wouldn't be able to ignore the feat of Arthur pulling the sword from the stone just after leaving the castle. The Duke would also no doubt consult Melora about the inability of everyone else to free the sword. If it were fate that Arthur be King, then the Duke would certainly want to be the first in the land to support him in word and deed.

Spurred by his newly restored self-confidence, Arthur told Merlin to remain outside while he spoke to the Duke alone. Arthur wished desperately to appear courageous and fearless, and Merlin's presence was protective and belittling. Merlin agreed, and watched the future king march with unmistakable determination up to the huge wooden doors. Without even a last turn to look at Merlin, Arthur grabbed the big iron knocker and banged on the door as if he would kick it down if it didn't open immediately. If Merlin could see the intensity in Arthur's blue eyes, that ferocious gaze, he would know that for the first time young Arthur truly believed he was a king.

After three steady bangs loud enough to rattle the walls in even the most remote corners of the castle, Arthur pushed his way in as fiercely as a conquering lord into the stronghold of the vanquished. He steeled himself as he went through the entrance, so that when he finally confronted the Duke, he would look every bit like the uncompromising king that he pretended to be. The fact that the Duke was sitting right there in the anteroom before a roaring fire drinking hot mead startled Arthur, but fortunately he had no time to react.

"You again? Why am I not surprised?"

"Then you've been expecting me," Arthur said presumptuously.

"That doesn't mean I've been looking forward to seeing you."

"I'll come right to the point. I'm here for your support in my ascension to the throne." Arthur extended his right hand. "Shake my hand and invite me to drink, and we'll toast our new alliance."

"I don't think so."

"I can't count on your undying loyalty?"

"No, now get out."

"But I am King, and I will be crowned."

"That's no concern of mine, little one. I've learned that by minding my own business out here and professing neither loyalty nor opposition to anyone, I'm beyond the petty schemes and machinations of the monarchy."

This was the one reaction that Arthur was unprepared for, and he had to stumble for a response. "Then... you don't care who's King?"

"Not in the least."

"Don't you want more power, lands and titles, like everyone else?"

"No, because then you have to maintain and defend them. If you have too much, someone is sure to try to take some of it away from you. If you do become King, let that be a lesson to you. Probably the most valuable one you'll ever learn."

Arthur shook his head woefully. "Boy, for a blackhearted tyrant, you sure don't live up to your reputation."

"That's the secret of my longevity, apathy. I ignore everyone and in turn, they ignore me. It's a beautiful arrangement. I suggest you try it, starting now."

Arthur placed his hands on his hips. "I shan't take no for an answer this time."

"Oh, you shan't, eh? Then allow me to persuade you." The Duke rose from his chair by the fire and picked Arthur up without warning in his huge black-gloved hands.

"Hey, put me down! I command you!"

"If I ever see you again I'll turn you over to Melora. And I promise that she'll be much less hospitable."

"You'll pay for this, you lout!"

The Duke didn't utter another word, but carried Arthur out the front entrance like a sack of old clothes. He walked him ten yards from the door and set him down with enough force to drive the long protruding sheath on Arthur's belt right into the hard ground. Merlin was too startled to move. He could only watch helplessly as Arthur was disposed of in the most ignoble manner imaginable. The Duke left the young king there, sticking out of the firm ground like a scarecrow hanging from his pole, only with his arms flailing and his mouth going.

"Wait! Come back here! I'll see you hanged! I'll cut your head off myself! This shall be the darkest day of your life, you scoundrel!" The doors of the castle slammed shut and Arthur stopped fighting, his whole body sagging with failure. "Merlin, help me," he whimpered finally.

Merlin came to his rescue and pulled the sheath out of the ground just as swiftly as Arthur had pulled the sword from the stone. "I'm so sorry, Sire. His reaction is most incomprehensible."

Arthur brushed himself off in disgust. "You no longer need to convince me, Merlin. I've no intention of giving up. A king takes what he wants, and accepts no defeat."

"Bravo!" Merlin cried as he watched Arthur run

back to the castle and throw himself at the door with all his strength. But the heavy wooden doors didn't give this time, for they were now barred to all invaders from inside. The Duke had made sure there would be no repeat encounter with the boy.

"What?! This is your King!" Arthur shouted indignantly as he pounded away. "I demand entrance this instant!"

Inside the castle, the Duke sat by the fire, with Melora nearby this time. He sighed with growing irritation. "I gave the whelp every chance. But he'll not be dissuaded, Melora." She laughed sinisterly.

"Why not make this easy. Let me turn him into a worm and then you can take him fishing." She laughed again, at her own malicious suggestion.

The Duke calmly sipped his mead as the pounding and protesting continued right outside. Then his eye caught the pewter goblet in his hand, and his face finally lit up. "No, let's be especially creative. We shall get rid of him and ensure that no one will ever darken my door again. Melora, I want you to send him to the place of my very last descendant. He wants to win someone over, then so be it. And if he succeeds, he'll be the greatest king the world has ever seen."

The Duke smiled confidently at this marvelous notion. Then he turned back to the fire and finished his drink.

10

think he's asleep."

"Then we should wake him up."

"He looks dead."

"He's not dead. I can see him breathing."

"He could just be passed out."

"Whadaya mean, just?"

"Yeah, then we should probably call an ambulance."

"Why's he dressed like that?"

"Maybe he was going to a Halloween party."

"It's the middle of September, stupid."

"Wake him up, Casey."

"Yeah, you saw him first. Wake him up."

"Okay, relax. Just stand back, so he doesn't freak out." Casey set the football on the ground and the small group of boys inched back a few steps. He knelt down beside Arthur, who was completely unconscious. "Hey, kid. Wake up." Arthur didn't move. His faced remained blank. Casey lightly placed his hand on Arthur's shoulder and shook him. "Hey, you okay? Come on, wake up."

"Hey, maybe he really is dead," Kevin repeated.

"Let's call the cops, just in case," Sean said. He was Kevin's younger brother, and he was always ready to call the cops.

"Shut up," Casey said evenly. "We're not callin' anybody yet." He shook him again, harder. "Hey! Wake up!" Casey shouted, giving it one last try.

Arthur stirred and groaned just loud enough to be heard.

"He's comin' around," Casey told them, relieved. He wasn't sure what he would've done otherwise. "Come on, kid! Get up!"

He shook him again, almost as hard, leaving his hand there.

Arthur opened his eyes. There was a peculiar object by his face. It was large, brown and egg-shaped. He didn't have any idea what it was. Then he realized that he didn't have any idea where he was. Arthur raised his head, then turned over and tried to sit up. His head throbbed and he held it with both hands. "Oh, my head. What happened?"

"I think he's okay," Casey announced.

The air smelled strange, he realized. The conflagration of dense odors invading Arthur's nose told him that he was far from home. He made a sour, disgusted face. Arthur inhaled, trying to qualify his impressions while searching for the familiar scent of the forest he knew.

Then Arthur remembered the Duke. "Merlin, what happened?" He looked around. There was no castle and no forest, only a small brick structure nestled among some bushes not far away.

But he was in a huge clearing completely surrounded by enormous trees. "Where am I?"

"Y'all right?" Casey asked, getting a strange
feeling about this kid.

Arthur noticed the group of boys staring down
at him. They all seemed about his age. "Who're
you?" he asked Casey, who was closest to him.
Casey was sandy haired and, except for his little
round, silver-framed glasses, physically similar to
Arthur.

"Who're you?" Kevin, a big, ruddy-faced boy,
demanded, as if that were the only sensible question. He stepped forward and snatched up the football. Kevin twirled it in his fleshy hands as he waited for a response.

Arthur's attention was drawn by the strange
brown ball. "What's that?"

"What?" Casey asked him.

Arthur pointed at the ball in Kevin's hands.
"That." He got up slowly, almost stumbling.

"Y'all right?"

"Yes. I just don't know what happened to me."

"You want us to call somebody? What's your
name?"

"Arthur."

"I'm Casey. This is Kevin, Sean and Mickey."
He signaled over his shoulder with his thumb, but
didn't really indicate who was who.

"Hello," Arthur replied absently while looking
around. "Where are we? Is this another part of the
forest?"

"The forest?" Kevin exclaimed. "This is Prospect

Park."

"Prospect Park," Arthur repeated slowly. "I'm unfamiliar with that part of the country. And you speak strangely. What part of England is this?"

"England?!" Kevin looked astonished. "This is Brooklyn."

"Brooklyn?"

"Yeah, Brooklyn, New York. Where'd you think?" He held the football up in front of Arthur's confused face. "And this is a football. Anything else you wanna know?" He shook his head. "What's with this kid?"

"Shut up, idiot. Maybe he's got amnesia."

"Huh?"

"He coulda been hit on the head. Y'ever think of that?"

Kevin didn't know what to say, and just stared at Arthur. "He knew his name," Sean said in his defense.

"Yeah," Kevin added defiantly.

"Can you remember where you live?" Casey asked gently.

"Yes, with Ector and my brother Kay. But I've spent most of my recent days with Merlin. Is he here, too?"

"Merlin," Casey repeated. "You mean like Merlin the magician?"

Arthur's face lit up. "You've heard of Merlin? Then I can't be too far from the forest."

"Now I'm sure we should call the cops," Sean said. "This kid's nuts."

"Sean," Casey scolded.

"He's gotta be jokin', Case," Mickey commented. "Like it's part of the costume." Mickey was small and wiry, with sharp, dark features. When he spoke it was always out the left side of his mouth.

"Yeah, why're you dressed like that?" Kevin asked. "You going' to a party or something?"

"A party? I don't understand you. I'm the new King of England. Since I pulled this sword from the stone in the forest. Have you not yet heard the news?"

"Oh, I get it," Mickey cried. "He's King Arthur, like in the story."

"Yeah," Kevin agreed.

"Yes, the story. Then you know of it."

"Sure. He's going' to a party as King Arthur," Mickey announced to the rest of them. "You're really convincing. This is the best costume I ever seen."

Casey said nothing. He just kept his eyes on Arthur. Somehow, he knew that he wasn't kidding or playing or going to any costume party.

"But this is no costume. I am King, as decreed by the freeing of the sword, which no one could do but me." Arthur had become indignant. He couldn't stand not to be taken seriously again. "You too, doubt my right to the throne?! Well I shan't be tolerant of this insolence any longer!" He stepped back and with one swift motion, pulled the sword from its sheath and brandished it before him.

The boys jumped back. "That thing looks real!" Kevin shouted.

"Take it easy," Casey said gently, trying to calm him down. He could see that Arthur was deadly serious.

"I shall dispatch the next poor fool to suggest that I'm not the true King."

"Relax. Put that down. No one's saying... you're not King Arthur."

Arthur relented at the title. The familiarity of the term in Casey's voice was bewildering. "King Arthur," he repeated to himself. He lowered the sword but kept both hands on it.

"Maybe this kid is nuts," Mickey whispered. "We should call somebody, Case."

"Don't worry, it's okay. You can trust us, Arthur. Okay?"

Arthur nodded firmly. "Agreed. Then we are all friends and allies." He sheathed the sword and stepped forward to shake each of their hands. The boys didn't have time to resist and complied without hesitation. But Kevin and Mickey smirked, and Sean had to suppress a laugh. Only Casey could look Arthur squarely in the face. He could see a gleam in Arthur's eye indicating the sincerity of his every word.

"Now what did you call that object?" Arthur asked, reaching for the football. "I've never seen anything like it."

"It's a football," Kevin told him again. "It's for a game we were playing."

"Ah." Arthur took the ball and twirled it in his hands, gazing at it wondrously.

"What're we gonna do with him, Case?" Mickey asked quietly. "There's really something wrong with him."

Casey turned so Arthur wouldn't hear him. "It's a fantasy world, 'cause he can't deal with reality."

"Why?"

"I don't know. He's probably got a bad home life. Maybe his parents fight and he just couldn't take it anymore."

"Yeah, I'll bet that's it," Sean said enthusiastically. "So what're we gonna do?"

"Well, we sure can't call the cops," Casey declared. "They'll just send him home."

Casey watched him toss the football in the air at Kevin's prompting. Despite Arthur's sudden outburst, he'd never seen anyone who looked so harmless and helpless. "He'll hafta come home with me, I guess."

"For how long?"

"I don't know. But if he's run away from home, he's gotta go somewhere."

"Won't your mom call the cops?" Mickey asked smartly.

Casey thought for a moment. "I'll just tell 'em he's new in school. That oughta give us a few days."

"A few days for what?"

"To find out who he is and where he lives." Casey turned to Arthur, who was now having a catch with Kevin from a few feet away.

"That's good," Kevin commented. "But try to hold it like this." He grasped the ball with his fingertips along the laces and tossed a perfect spiral into Arthur's cradled arms.

"Why's it called a football, if our feet have yet to touch it?"

"I dunno, Arthur. It just is."

"Hey Arthur, we hafta go home now. You wanna come to my house for a while?"

"Well, I should really look for Merlin. But since I'm not familiar with this region, perhaps it best if I remain with the lot of you for the time being."

"Great, let's go." Casey started walking towards the outskirts of the park, and Arthur and the other boys followed.

"Do you know just how far I am from England?"

"Far."

"Too far to walk?"

Casey nodded. "No one can walk from Brooklyn to England. Not even King Arthur."

II

he boys passed a large pond surrounded by tall reeds and covered with algae, then drifted across Long Meadow towards the bushy oak and elm trees that bordered the park. As they went, Casey noticed that Arthur was exceptionally distracted by the other groups of people nearby. To one side some men played soccer, and to the other, at the end of the expanse, a number of baseball and softball games went on. When they passed a pair of families having a picnic, Arthur was compelled to stop and stare at the strange sight.   Casey pulled him along and explained what they were doing.

Arthur said, "Curious," with all sincerity, and couldn't help himself from glancing back a few times. Casey was glad that the tree tops concealed Grand Army Plaza, with its massive white arch and giant bronze war memorial. He couldn't imagine what Arthur would've made of that astonishing sight, or the distant skyscrapers of Manhattan, for that matter. Then again, Casey reasoned, it might be just the thing to snap him out of it.

When they emerged from the lush enclave on Prospect Park West and Ninth Street they were suddenly on the streets of Brooklyn. As they walked west, Arthur was met with the noise and activity of a modern city, a place he could never have imagined, and in which he was set adrift without cause or warning. What had happened in the forest and what was he doing in this strange place? He stopped short when he saw the cars and the tall buildings, and how everyone was dressed. "Ah," he exclaimed. "Now I see the sense of it."

"What, Arthur?" Casey asked.

"This cannot be the world I know. I have been sent into the future by Melora, the Duke's haggard old witch. He's sure to be free of me now."

Kevin rolled his eyes, then looked at Casey as if he were now solely responsible for Arthur. "You're really gonna bring this kid home?"

"Just don't tell anybody about him, awright? I'll give 'em some of my clothes and get him to act normal." As they approached 6th Avenue, Casey slowed down. He wasn't sure if this was going to work and he wasn't too eager to get home.

"Good luck. What about Cathy? She'll know something's up right off."

"Don't worry, he'll just seem a little weird. It's not like she's gonna think he's really... who he says."

"I don't know. It sounds like you're gonna get caught, no matter what."

"Yeah," Sean agreed. "Your parents'll just end up calling the cops anyway."

"Can't you shut up about the cops for five minutes!" They stopped at the corner when they reached 6th Avenue. "I'll see you guys tomorrow. Come on, Arthur. We have to go this way." He turned downtown, walking towards the edge of Park Slope.

Arthur turned to the rest of them. "Farewell, then. I hope it shan't be long before we meet again."

"Yeah, maybe in school tomorrow. 'Bye, Arthur." Kevin waved goodbye, prompting Sean and Mickey to say goodbye and do the same.

Arthur followed his new friend down 6th Avenue, the sun glinting oddly off his armor and his huge sword dragging along the sidewalk like an aluminum baseball bat. Casey noticed the constant stares on the way, but tried to ignore them for Arthur's sake. He became progressively aware of the scraping sound of Arthur's sword, which seemed to be the loudest thing on the street and attracted even more attention than his armor. Casey wondered how Arthur could be so obviously out of place and still walk along calmly. He was waiting for Arthur to slip up, and acknowledge that he was aware of his own masquerade. Casey would glance at him every few seconds. But so far, Arthur had not betrayed himself even unconsciously.

"How did you say you got here?" Casey asked to keep Arthur talking about himself.

"Melora, the Duke's old witch. Her magic's the

most powerful in the land. Merlin could do nothing to stop it."

"I thought Merlin was one of the greatest wizards ever."

"Not the Merlin I know. He's only been a wizard a short time. Can't turn himself into anything, doesn't understand the meaning of his visions, and he didn't even know what the sword in the stone was for." Arthur shook his head. "Now I'm stuck here, so far from my homeland and the things I know that I may never get back. Some king, eh?" Arthur stared at the ground dejectedly.

For the moment, Casey couldn't dispute a word of it, and found himself laying a sympathetic hand on Arthur's drooping shoulder. "Don't worry, Arthur. We'll find a way to get you back. I promise."

Arthur picked his head up and managed to smile.

Casey stopped at the next corner, where they faced a busy intersection. Arthur stopped and watched cars speed past them in different directions. For the first time he noticed that there were people in them. "These are the strangest carriages," he said.

"What, the cars?"

"Cars," he repeated. "Have you no horses?"

"Horses, no. They go on their own. But sometimes the cops use horses for patrol."

"Cops?"

"Yeah, you know." As Arthur stared at him, Casey realized that he'd never had to think about exactly what the police did. "They uh... enforce the law."

"Ah, like knights. They must carry swords, too." He patted his own, hanging from his belt and still dragging on the sidewalk.

"No, they carry guns," Casey said as the light changed. He stepped off the curb and led Arthur across 3rd Street. Then he realized that he would have to explain this as well. "They shoot chunks of lead that can kill you real easy."

"I'd surely like to see that."

"Look, we gotta stay away from the cops. They'll take you in and then you'll hafta... " Casey shut himself up when he realized just what he was about to say. "They can't help you, okay?" Casey pointed up ahead. "My house is just around the corner." Casey was looking forward to getting off such a main street, where there were so many people to stare at Arthur as they went by.

"Hey, that's some costume!" a voice shouted suddenly. "Who's that, Hanson?"

"Oh no." He knew it was too good to be true. Why couldn't it be somebody they could just ignore?

A tall, lean figure stepped out into their path. It was Frank Mayo. He was a few years older than Casey and had been giving him a hard time ever since his sister Cathy had decided that she couldn't stand him. He couldn't pick on her, so he took his vengeance out on Casey whenever he ran into him. He usually hung out in front of the Italian American Grocery a few blocks over, on Union

Street in Carroll Gardens, Mickey and Kevin's neighborhood. Mayo was three feet away from them, and there was no way to avoid him.

"Where's the party and why wasn't I invited?" he said with a smirk.

"There's no party, Frank," Casey muttered and kept walking.

"Hey, I's talkin' to you!"

Casey stopped and turned around. "What?"

"Who's he anyway? I never seen him around anywhere."

"He's not from around here, okay?"

Frank stepped towards Arthur and flicked at his purple tunic dismissively. "What's all this, huh?"

"Just leave him alone. He's... my cousin, Artie."

Frank took hold of Arthur's shoulder and looked at him critically. "What's he retarded or something?"

Arthur abruptly shook himself loose. "Unhand me, you wretch. Or't shall be your last act on this Earth." Before Casey could react, Arthur unsheathed his sword and swung it up to the level of Frank's exposed white neck.

"Arthur, no!"

Frank was bug-eyed. He was never so scared in his life. "G-get him off," he whispered desperately.

"Arthur, relax. He's always saying dumb things like that."

"I should dispatch him for his insolence."

"Yeah, I know. We'd all like to, but it's not worth

the trouble. Come on, let's just go home."

Arthur hesitated, then lowered his sword. But he continued to glare at Frank, preventing him from moving or even blinking.

"Very well. But remain on your guard, man."

"Yeah, sure. No problem."

As they got to Garfield Place and turned the corner, Casey couldn't help smiling as he cautioned Arthur about his second sudden outburst in the last fifteen minutes. He'd finally seen Frank Mayo get what he deserved, but he was now even more worried about Arthur's behavior. If he were this hard to control, whether he had a sword in his hand or not, he was going to get himself in serious trouble in no time.

"Back home, such a knave would find himself cut in small pieces before he could say a word."

"Well I think you shut him up for a while. But listen to me, okay? You gotta promise you'll just be careful. If there'd been cops around, that'd be it. Nobody walks around with swords around here and duels out in the street like that."

"Really? How do you solve your differences?"

"Well, usually we just work them out by talking. We try to avoid bloodshed."

"Seems like an invitation to so much unfinished business to me. I gathered that you'd had unpleasant dealings with the oaf before. If you'd merely dispatched him at your first confrontation, the problem would be solv'd."

"Yeah, but he could've just as easily done the same to me."

Arthur nodded reluctantly. "Yes, I see the sense of it. But we should remain vigilant just the same, should he return with some of his compatriots with revenge in his heart."

"That's probably a good idea," Casey allowed as they stopped in front of the fifth house in on the small quiet street. "Here we are Arthur. Now we hafta get upstairs to my room before anybody sees us."

"Why?"

"'Cause we hafta get you out of those clothes and into something normal. We also need an explanation for you."

"I thought you'd decided that I'm a visiting cousin."

"My parents already know all my cousins, Arthur."

12

asey swiftly led Arthur up the stairs of the narrow brick house. He usually went around the block, through the alley to the back of the house and in through the kitchen door. But the front door was much closer to the stairs to the second floor, where his bedroom was. Casey unlocked the front door and opened it cautiously. Since it was Sunday, he knew that somebody had to be home. He immediately heard sounds in the kitchen, and spotted his father in the living room, his head hidden behind the Sunday sports section of the newspaper.

"That you, Case?"

"Uh, yeah Dad." With a finger over his lips, he motioned to Arthur to come in quietly. Together they slipped upstairs with barely a sound and barricaded themselves in his bedroom.

Arthur looked around curiously. "These are indeed strange cottages. But they do seem warm and comfortable."

The clutter of Casey's room immediately reminded Arthur of Merlin's cottage. It was crammed with numerous objects, and there were books and papers everywhere and large pictures on the walls. The bed was unmade and clothes were all over the floor. On one side of the small room a flat surface was covered with dark, oblong items, dazzling Arthur with an endless array of lights, dials and buttons. Casey went over to one of them and flipped a switch, turning on the stereo. He raised the music's volume just enough to drown out their voices. Arthur looked around, confused by the sudden rush of aggressive sounds filling the room.

"My sister Cathy's probably home, too. It's almost dinner time. She's always poking her nosy head in here, so we gotta get things together quick."

"You each have your own bed chamber?"

"What? Oh, yeah."

"A small castle, this. At home there's only two rooms, front and back."

"Well, this place isn't really that big. We're not rich or anything, like some kids I know from school."

"Dinner's almost ready, Case, so get washed up!" Casey looked stricken as his father's voice boomed from downstairs.

"Come on, we gotta get you outa those clothes."

"Then I'm to look like you for the rest of my time here?"

"Well you sure can't go around in a suit of armor and a sword on your belt."

"But I'd feel naked with no sword. I'm hardly a king without it."

"As soon as somebody spots it, they're gonna wonder who you are. Hiding you's gonna be tough enough as it is. We can't take any chances, Arthur."

Arthur nodded. "Yes, I see. Merlin always said that a careful guarding of the truth is the best course to follow. It still prevails in this day and age."

"Yeah yeah, just come on," Casey said nervously.

Arthur undid his belt and proceeded to discard the heavy chain mail, which he hadn't had off since Merlin had first put him in it. "Ah, what a relief. I forgot what such freedom of movement was like." Arthur waved his arms up and down like he expected to float off the ground.

Casey groaned. Arthur was somewhat scrawny, and more than a little dirty. The only recourse under the circumstances was his first modern shower and a quick lesson in adolescent grooming.

"Are you sure such drastic measures are necessary?" Arthur asked after Casey's emphatic recommendation.

"You wanna fit in, don't you? Believe me, Arthur, you'll not only look modern, you'll even feel modern. Let's go into the bathroom."

"The bathroom," he repeated ominously. The very word sounded vile and unpleasant.

Casey opened the bathroom door and stood by the entrance like Virgil at the gates of hell. Arthur peered in timidly. He saw nothing recognizable. Surely this was some modern torture chamber from which he'd never escape. Casey ushered him in with gentle tones. "There's nothing to be afraid of, believe me."

When Arthur found himself in the small clean room crowded with strange shiny fixtures, the mirror was the only thing that he trusted. "Ah, a looking glass. Never have I seen one of such clarity and brilliance."

Casey settled in behind Arthur and looked at his reflection.

"There, see how dirty and messy you are. We gotta get you cleaned up, or everyone'll notice that too."

Arthur noticed all manner of tubes and containers on the sink and picked them up in succession. "Are these magic cleaning potions?"

"Yeah, but you don't need them yet. Soap and shampoo come first. Come on, get into the shower." Casey leaned over and turned on the water, which shot out of the shower head with such force that Arthur jumped back suddenly.

"'Tis only water, but how does it come through the wall like that?" He reached in and let it run over his hand. "And so warm and clean! What a marvel!"

"Arthur, you gotta stop being amazed at everything or we'll never get through the day. Now in you go." Casey exhaled heavily. He'd been with Arthur less than an hour and he was already exhausted from all the teaching and explaining and warning, which he began to fear would never end. All at once, Casey understood what his parents had gone through until recently with him and his sister, and it gave him a sudden jolt of gratitude and admiration for them. So this is what it's like to have kids, he thought.

Arthur enjoyed the stream of hot water running over his head and down his body. Indeed, he'd never felt anything like it. He could have stood motionless under it forever, had Casey not been there prodding him with instructions every few seconds. He told him how to use the soap and wash his hair with shampoo, which he made him do twice. He handed him a washcloth and made sure that he scrubbed the back of his neck and behind his ears. Then, just when Arthur was ready for more, he suddenly turned off he water, which startled Arthur and made him feel cold. He tossed him a clean towel after he stepped out of the shower and showed him how to vigorously dry himself off and comb his hair, which was now a few shades lighter.

"Okay, good. But you should probably brush your teeth now, too."

"My teeth? You clean them as well?"

"Yup, definitely a good idea, since you probably haven't seen a toothbrush in a while."

"Come on Casey, what're you doing in there?!" It was Cathy, critical and scolding as usual. She'd pushed open the bedroom door and was now on her way towards the bathroom.

"Great, my sister." With only a split second to think, Casey opened the bathroom door before she could reach it and stuck just his head out from behind it. "What?!"

She stopped in her tracks, and folded her arms

in front of her. "Dinner's almost ready. Didn't you hear Mom calling?"

"I was in the shower, okay?"

"In the middle of the day?" She was immediatcly suspicious. No fourteen year old boy took a shower unless his mother forced him, and not on a Sunday afternoon.

"I was playing football in the park. I's covered with mud. Ya mind?"

She smirked. "Hm." Casey could see the wheels turning already. "Okay, but you better come down quick." She turned, the smirk still in place, and went out of the room.

Casey didn't make a sound until he heard her feet on the stairs. "Whoa, that was close. Good thing I hid your sword and stuff in the closet or we'd be doomed. We're gonna hafta really be on our toes with her around."

Arthur nodded. "Aye, the relentless curiosity of women is well-known from horizon to horizon, in every century."

"Now, let's get your teeth brushed and get outa here before someone else decides to visit."

When Arthur finished, Casey rushed him out of the bathroom and into one of his T-shirts, with a New York Giants sweatshirt over it, a pair of jeans, clean socks and an old pair of sneakers that he hadn't had the heart to throw away. He told Arthur to try to act as much like him and his friends as possible, and proceeded to lead him downstairs.

"Okay, this is it," Casey warned them both as they reached the kitchen and the moment of truth.

13

asey's father sat at the kitchen table, still hidden by the newspaper. His mother stood at the stove, cooking and stirring.

She turned and when the two boys entered the kitchen. Casey watched his mother's face for a reaction to Arthur. When she didn't seem shocked or surprised, he dared to think that maybe there was nothing peculiar about him.

"Everybody, this is Arthur, Arthur... uh King. He's just moved here from England."

"Well, isn't that interesting," said Casey's mother.

"He was playing football with us in the park."

"American football," his father added, finally putting the paper aside. "Their football is our soccer, eh Arthur?"

"Soccer?" Arthur looked confused again.

"He's staying for dinner, isn't he Casey?"

"Oh yeah, Mom. Sure." Casey had figured that his mother would invite Arthur to stay since they were just about to eat. This was the one thing he'd counted on. It saved him the trouble of having to ask his parents if Arthur could stay, which was important considering that there was nowhere for Arthur to go.

"Providing his parents know where he is."

"Oh yeah, they do. He told them he wouldn't be home until later."

"Okay. But he can use the phone if he wants."

"No, that's okay."

"Where'd *he* come from?" Cathy asked suspiciously. She'd been sitting at the table, staring at Arthur the whole time.

"What? He was in my room."

"I didn't see him when I was up there."

"He musta been in the closet, looking for a sweatshirt. He tore his in the park."

"Mm." Cathy continued to stare dubiously. "Arthur King," she said slowly, as if examining the name.

Casey's mother came to the table carrying a large serving plate with steaming heaps of corned beef and cabbage. Casey was relieved. This looked pretty safe.

"I hope you like corned beef, Arthur."

"Too bad he's not Irish, dear. If we'd known you were coming, we'd have had roast beef instead." Casey's father laughed.

"The Irish are a vile lot, sir. No King of England shall ever be Irish."

Casey nearly went ghost white. He now feared that the meal would be an unstoppable disaster, for if Arthur could say nothing that weren't a reference to his pretended medieval home, he'd sound completely out of his mind by the end of the evening.

Casey's father grinned. "That's for sure. Just be careful how you joke about them around here, the neighborhood's half Irish."

"Then you've been overrun with them, the vermin."

"Oh boy." Casey forced himself to laugh. "Uh, Kevin and Sean were giving him a hard time about being English. I guess all that kidding's hard to stop. Okay, Arthur, don't get carried away. It's getting old." Casey looked at him sternly, hoping he would take the hint.

"Aye, at least they're not as bad as the Scots. They rub mud all over their faces before they go into battle, to scare their enemies. And they blow those infernal pipes to unnerve them as well."

"Arthur's... a big medieval history buff," Casey explained with a grin.

"Well he sounds right at home with that subject," Casey's father replied. "The Civil War's my area, Arthur. I can't get enough of it." He proceeded to dole out portions of corned beef and cabbage with a large serving fork.

"Anything to drink, Arthur?" Casey's mother asked pleasantly.

"Have you any ale, madam?"

Casey's eyes went wide with horror. God, what a nightmare, he thought. What was I thinking?

"Ginger ale? I think we do." She went to the kitchen and rooted around in the crowded refrigerator. "Here we go." She poured a glass of ginger ale and set it on the table in front of Arthur.

Arthur took a sip and seemed satisfied. "Mm, this is quite good," he concluded heartily.

"Well, thank you."

Casey relaxed slightly. It was another hurdle, but he didn't know how much more he could take of this waiting for a disaster that just couldn't be laughed off or explained away. Casey had assumed there was a limit to Arthur's medieval behavior. He'd thought that it would be too difficult for him to keep up the charade. But with every obscure reference, it was apparent that there was no end to Arthur's belief that he was truly the thousand year old King of England. He'd yet to betray himself with even the smallest understanding of modern life, and Casey was beginning to doubt that there was much hope of his recognizing anything from now on.

When they started eating there was another cause for alarm that made Casey forget all the previous ones. As he, Cathy and their parents reached for their forks, Arthur's hand went right for the mound of corned beef on his plate. In an instant, Casey realized that eating with a knife and fork was as foreign to the medieval world as a pair of chopsticks. In true form, Arthur was ready to pick up that pile of meat and stuff it right into his gaping mouth.

Without even thinking, Casey dropped his fork and grabbed Arthur's wrist in mid-air. No one noticed, and Casey whispered, "Fork," then nodded quickly to the fork sitting on a napkin next to his plate. He guided his hand to it and Arthur picked it up, unsure of its purpose. Casey picked up his again and demonstrated discreetly, then he locked eyes with Arthur so desperately to prompt its imitation, that Arthur kept it up and mimicked him throughout the entire meal, motion-for-motion.

When Casey's parents noticed the practice, they thought it was a game, which he encouraged by smiling and glancing at Arthur as if he were in on the joke. But Cathy's reaction was a little different. After a typically snide scolding to stop fooling around, she spent the meal glaring suspiciously at Casey, making him realize that *she* knew there was something funny going on.

Casey just wanted to get through the meal, so he could get Arthur back up to his room and give him a crash course in how to act normal and not stand out. Meanwhile, he made sure to speak for Arthur whenever he could, and qualified his answers to his parents' casual questions. But it was Casey who kept tripping up. He had to lie about where Arthur lived, what his parents did, how he liked America, what his favorite school subjects were, and why he didn't seem to know anything about sports, books, movies, TV shows, cars or anything else in which teenage boys were supposed to have an interest.

Cathy kept her participation to a minimum. But Casey knew his sister better than he knew anybody. Her reaction to Arthur's presence was unmistakable. Whenever she glanced at him and then at Casey, he knew for sure that she couldn't wait to make trouble for both of them.

14

asey hurried Arthur back up to his room as soon as dinner was over. When he shut the door behind them, he was never so relieved in his life. "Finally," he exhaled, and flopped down on his bed. "Arthur, you can't leave this room until we can figure out a way for you to avoid sounding ridiculous every time you open your mouth."

"I don't understand, Casey. I thought we all got on quite well at dinner."

"Well think again. What was all that stuff about the Scots and the Irish and the English? This is America. It's full of different kinds of people."

"Aren't you all Americans?"

"Well yeah, we are, but... just about everybody's grandparents or great grandparents are from somewhere else."

"Where?"

Casey sat up on the bed, crossways, with his back against the wall. "Europe mostly. Italy,

Ireland, Germany. But a lotta other places, too. Like Russia, China, Mexico, Puerto Rico, Denmark."

"Ah, now I understand."

"Good."

"We were nearly overrun by the Danes ourselves. The Nordic scum took over half the British Isles."

"Arthur, *my* great grandparents were from Denmark."

"They didn't come here to conquer and rule by force?"

"No, they were just poor dairy farmers. They came for freedom and a better life."

Arthur narrowed his eyes and pursed his lips. The notion sounded suspicious, if not downright unnatural. "People leaving their own countries. I cannot even imagine it. I'm as English as the dirt under my feet there." He made a fist and frowned with disgust. "I shall never leave it, nor will it ever leave me."

"Yeah, well okay, but... I guess it's just a different world now. But promise me you won't mention how people look or where they're from or any of that, 'cause you'll get beat up."

Arthur jumped to his feet. "I shan't shrink from any contest with any man!" he shouted with raw indignation. "Where is my sword? I've been separated from it for too long."

Casey put his head in his hands and groaned. "No sword, awright?! Arthur, that's what I'm talking about. We don't want you getting into any fights. It's too risky. You hafta try not to be too noticeable. Just fit in and keep quiet, understand?"

"I shall try, Casey. For I trust you and know you would not lead me astray."

"That's another thing. You can't talk like that."

"What's wrong with the manner in which I talk?"

Casey just stared at him. This is gonna take real work, he thought. "It's too... direct and formal. Try to be more relaxed and casual, you know?"

Arthur nodded. "That I can do."

"Just say 'okay' and 'yeah' if you agree with something. And 'nah' or 'forget it' if you disagree. Anymore than that sounds weird."

Arthur sighed. "'Tis not much like a king I fear."

"But nobody's supposed to know you're a king. Pretend to be like everybody else for a while. You might even like it."

"Yes, that may be valuable. A king must know the soul of the people if he's to be a true king."

"Good, keeping thinking that way. We got alot more to worry about here. Like where you're gonna stay and what you're gonna do while me and the guys're in school tomorrow."

"I can't stay here with you?" Arthur looked down at Casey, and all the menace and pride left his face. He gazed into Casey's eyes waiting for a response, his own eyes clear and blue with true innocence.

"Well it's not that simple." Casey felt bad. For all of Arthur's weirdness and confusion, he seemed genuinely baffled by the possibility of his expulsion. "See, it's a school night. Nobody can stay over or anything. Besides, you're supposed to live around here somewhere and should just be able to go home yourself."

"But I don't have anywhere to go. And if I'm to find out why I'm here and how I can get back to my real home, I'll need some time. I have to sleep somewhere."

"I know, I know." Casey looked around the room hopelessly.

He knew that he couldn't just kick Arthur out. He was responsible for him now. More than that, Casey realized that he couldn't let him out of his sight. He didn't trust him to fit in well enough, and he sure didn't trust Brooklyn.

"Have you no barns or stables?" Arthur pleaded.

Casey shook his head. "No. The problem's not where. It's my parents and my sister finding out. There's no reason for you to stay here, so if they find you we'll have to tell the truth."

"Yes, I see. The risk is great. If only we could just tell them of the Duke and the witch Melora, who sent me here."

"Well we can't, since nobody believes in witches anymore."

"No witches? Such a thing is inconceivable. What do you all believe in then?"

"Science."

"What's that?"

"It's the study of the way things work. The forces of nature and stuff."

"Ah, alchemy. Merlin was interested in such principles when we first met, but he'd yet to master them."

Casey sighed and came to a decision. The fact that it was the only alternative didn't make it any easier. "Okay, you'll just have to stay here with me."

"In your house?"

"In my room. But we'll hafta make everyone think you went home. And then we'll hafta be real quiet."

"Agreed. What's your plan?"

If it weren't a Sunday night, there'd be no problem in having Arthur stay. Casey's bed even had a second fold-out bed built into it in case anybody slept over. But as long as Casey's parents thought Arthur was gone and Casey was up in his room alone, they wouldn't check up on him the rest of the night. After waiting until about nine o'clock, which was the usual time for Casey's friends to go home, Casey and Arthur went downstairs and walked into the kitchen. Casey made a show of saying goodbye to Arthur, with plenty of so-longs and see-you-tomorrows for all in the house to hear. Then he let Arthur out the back door and noisily closed it and locked it behind him.

Casey slowly went back to the stairs, just in time for Arthur to open the unlocked front door, and quietly follow him back upstairs to his room. They had even made sure to climb them in perfect unison, so they would sound like one person. Casey led Arthur back into his room in perfect silence and closed the door. He turned his music on low so it would cover their whispers, and set up the second bed for Arthur to sleep on. He was never so nervous in his life. It was as if he'd sneaked a girl up there. But if they were quiet, no one would discover them. Fortunately, every bedroom had its own bathroom, so there was no chance of any surprises there.

In the rest of the time before they went to sleep, Casey told Arthur about school and what he could expect there. He'd decided to take Arthur to school, and intended to register him as his visiting cousin, so he wouldn't have to sneak him in. With the vague resemblance, their being related wasn't out of the question. He also told him about Brooklyn, and what they could do after school let out. Arthur was eager to get there and see the other boys from the park, and also pursue his first full day of investigation. He wanted to explore his new surroundings and figure out why he was there and how he could get back. Casey told him that he would help him in every way he could, and was just as excited about getting started himself.

Before they finally went to sleep, Casey went downstairs to the kitchen to get them each a glass of water. He spotted the telephone book when he closed the refrigerator door, and it gave him an idea. He opened it to the K's and searched for the name King. There were hundreds of them in the Brooklyn area. He'd thought that he could call around and ask if they had a missing child, but there were far too many. Casey had to ask himself whether he was going to continue to humor Arthur, or whether he was going to find out his real identity. But so far, he hadn't even begun to challenge Arthur about who he was and where he was really from.

With everything he told Arthur, he was allowing him to further hide himself from discovery. This also meant by Arthur himself. Casey remembered something that his aunt had once said. She was a social worker and dealt with a lot of confused and crazy people in her job. You should never give in to someone's fantasies. It can be permanently destructive. The last two words were hers exactly, and Casey recalled her stern expression and serious tone.

He was really scared now. He'd hoped to somehow coax Arthur back to normal by bringing out small aspects of his real self. But Casey still hadn't seen any. Arthur's accent, mannerisms, reactions and responses were all perfect, as if he truly knew nothing of this world and this time. Casey went back upstairs, a bit more nervous than when he'd come down. He would have to decide soon. He didn't believe that the real King Arthur was up there in his room. But he didn't quite not believe it either.

15

W hen he woke up on Monday morning, Casey realized that getting Arthur out of the house would be a problem. He and Cathy always left for school just before his parents went to work. There was no way for him to pretend that it was like any other day without leaving Arthur behind. Casey also couldn't leave with Cathy, since it would allow her to find out that Arthur had stayed overnight. If he'd realized it the night before, he would have set his alarm for an hour earlier so he could get Arthur out of the house before everyone else got downstairs.

Casey sat at the kitchen table eating breakfast, his eyes drifting from one family member to the next as he tried to figure a way out of this crucial dilemma. The front door wasn't visible from the kitchen, but there was no way for Casey to signal Arthur to leave his room and sneak out.

"What're you kids doing after school?" Casey's mother asked.

"I'm gonna show Arthur around town," he said automatically.

"Oh, he's still not familiar with the neighborhood?"

"Uh, not really."

"Maybe we should invite his parents over for dinner," she said, thinking out loud.

"Mm," Casey's father said in vague agreement.

Oh great, he thought. Something else to worry about. Sorry folks, Arthur's parents can't make it 'cause he's really King Arthur and they haven't traveled with him to the twenty-first century. He had to get out of there before they started asking him questions about Arthur's parents or suggested that he invite them over the next time he saw them.

"I gotta go," Casey said and stood up like he was suddenly in a rush. "I left one of my books at Kevin's."

"Why can't he bring it to you at school?" Cathy asked nosily.

"He doesn't know it's there."

"Just call him now."

"He'll forget." Casey scurried back upstairs and was back down in a few moments with his coat and bookbag. He stopped on the last step and peered around the corner into the kitchen. Everyone was still at the table. It was now or never. He signaled to Arthur at the top of the landing and down he came. Casey opened the front door and out they went. He didn't stop or look back, and he hoped that no one wondered why he hadn't used the back door like always.

"Come on." Casey walked as fast as he could. He wanted them to get as far from the house as possible in the next few minutes. He didn't think anyone was following them, but he didn't want to relax and walk normally until they were completely safe. Casey took no chances and even followed a different route to school. Instead of walking down 5th Avenue and going west on Baltic, he led Arthur along Garfield until they hit Carroll Street. He didn't want Cathy to catch up to them or risk one of his parents passing them on the way to work.

"Okay," he said, finally slowing the pace. "Nobody'll run into us now. I don't know how we're gonna do this every day, Arthur. It's getting to me already."

Arthur nodded. "Then it's essential that I find my way back as soon as I can."

They walked on, but the neighborhood remained mostly the same. Like Casey's, the houses were three and four-story brownstones, and he explained that two families lived in many of them. As they passed the rows of modest brick and limestone houses, Arthur became intrigued by the large numbers on each building and started to announce them out loud.

"383... 375... 366... 352... "

"Those're the addresses," Casey said. "So you know where you live."

"Interesting."

"The mailman also needs them, for letters and stuff."

"I thought they were just strange signs, to keep count of all the houses."

Casey laughed. "When I was little my mom told me they were signs. Remember the sign outside our house she always said." As they approached the corner of Nevins, the front door to one of the houses opened and a pretty young girl came out. A red scarf held back her long dark hair, and perfectly matched her bookbag. Around her slender neck was a small cross on a fine gold chain. Casey recognized her from school. They were even in the same class.

"Hi, Theresa."

"Casey?" She came down her front steps, looking at him curiously. "What're you doing going this way?"

He had no explanation, but blurted out, "I had to pick up my cousin Arthur. He's just moved here from England."

Theresa looked at Arthur and smiled. "Oh, hi. I'm Theresa."

Arthur grinned in Casey's direction. "She's a fair wench, no?"

Oh God, here we go again, Casey thought.

"Wench?!" Her mouth hung open in disbelief.

"He's just kiddin' around Theresa. Knock it off, Arthur."

"I thought everybody in England was real polite."

"To women, we give a harsh word and a firm hand. 'Tis only a princess who deserves such courtesy."

"Arthur!" Casey was helpless. This was the one area of behavior that he'd forgot to mention last night. Now it was too late to give Arthur even a crash course in how to treat modern girls.

Theresa just stared at him. Even the dumbest jock in school had never spoken to her like this. Without thinking, she slapped his face as hard as she could. It was the first time she'd ever struck another person. "Your cousin's a real jerk. I'll have my big brother teach him a lesson if he ever talks to me again." She stalked off down the street.

"Spirited, but the maid should know her place." Arthur held his red cheek, leering at her as she marched away.

"Oh no!" Casey didn't know Theresa that well, but he didn't hesitate to chase after her. This was a disaster in the making, and he had to stop it immediately. "Wait, Theresa wait!"

"Go away!"

As Casey caught up to her he could see that she was almost in tears. If he couldn't somehow get her to stop and listen to reason right now, the incident would be all over school by lunch time and Arthur would get more attention than if he did tell everyone that he was the King of England. "Theresa, stop! Come on, please!"

Suddenly she halted and turned around. Her expression was scary and it almost took the nerve right out of him. He'd never seen anyone look so hurt and angry in his life. "What?" she spat. It couldn't have been worse if Casey himself had insulted her.

"I'm really sorry, okay. But listen, Arthur's not my cousin and he doesn't live around here."

"What?" Now she looked even madder. "Is this a big joke?"

"No, it's real serious. You gotta let me explain, okay?" He glanced back at Arthur, who hadn't moved from his spot.

"Casey?" Arthur called.

Casey's hand shot up. "Just stay there, Arthur!"

Theresa was getting annoyed. "Well?"

Casey looked at her and exhaled. There was no other way. "We found him in the park yesterday. Me and a few other guys."

"Found him?" She turned her head sharply to look at Arthur.

Casey lowered his voice. "He said he was King Arthur, and he had a whole costume and sword and everything."

"What?!"

"Shh. Listen, huh. I figure he's convinced himself 'cause he can't face going home. I think it's a real bad situation, and this's the only way he can deal with it."

"Didn't you tell someone?"

"No, not even my parents. The first thing they'll do is send him home."

"What about a doctor?"

Casey shook his head. "It's too risky."

"Where's he live?"

"I don't know. I don't anything about him, that's the whole point. If I can just find out a little about him, I can probably help him."

"He must be in real bad shape then."

"Yeah, that's what I'm afraid of. He's so deep into this fantasy that he might not be able to get out of it. Look how he talked to you. Did he seem like he was kidding?"

Theresa shook her head vehemently. "No, not at all." She kept looking at Arthur, who stood half a block away, like a lost dog who didn't know where to go.

"So now I'm stuck with him."

"You're bringin' him to school?"

"Yeah, I sure can't leave him at home." Casey looked at Arthur gravely. "Maybe he'll see something and snap out of it."

"Yeah, I hope so."

He turned back to Theresa and looked at her squarely. "Anyway, you can't tell anybody. And just act normal around Arthur. You gotta kinda humor him."

She nodded. "Okay. But I never heard of anything like this before. It sounds weird. There could be something really wrong with him, like a brain tumor or something." She turned and looked back at Arthur as if he might keel over and die on the spot.

"I know, but I still gotta look out for him." Casey turned and waved Arthur forward. "Come on, we're gonna be late for school!"

"I fear I've said the wrong thing again," he admitted when he caught up to them.

"Don't worry, I explained things to Theresa.

She understands you now."

"Ah, then the nymph is not immune to my advances." He glanced at Theresa with a smirk.

"Arthur!" Casey was about to scold him again, but Theresa stepped in.

"Wait a minute." She put a sympathetic hand on Arthur's arm. "Arthur, listen to me, okay. You can't talk to girls like that. It's mean, and it makes you look stupid. If I was your sister, would you want other boys to be mean to me?"

"As my sister, you'd be a most precious thing. I'd forbid you from talking to any boys at all."

"If you're good enough to talk to some girl, then they're good enough to talk to me."

"But no one wants other boys talking to his sister."

"But every girl is someone's sister or daughter."

Arthur didn't like the sound of this. "Then we must all talk to you and treat you nice, or none of us can talk to any of you."

She nodded emphatically. "That's right."

He thought this over uncomfortably. It just didn't seem right somehow. "Hm." He remembered how the knights would shout praises at the maidens they passed in the village, and sometimes carry them off on their horses. Their mothers would cry for a day or so, but it was considered a great honor to be chosen by a knight. "Then we can't have our way with you?" he concluded.

"No, of course not! You must talk to us nicely and take us places and give us things and treat us gently, like you're afraid we won't like you."

Arthur stepped back and looked her up and down in complete disbelief. Then he turned to Casey. "Is this true?! You actually behave this way?"

"I'm afraid so," he admitted gravely.

He still couldn't quite fathom it. "You woo them with gifts and flattery and all manner of sweet talk? You seek to win their favor like ladies at court?"

"Yes," Theresa insisted. "We want to be court-ed, because we don't deserve any less. It's the least you can do for someone's sister."

Arthur sighed, still deeply considering the bizarre notion. After a while he began to nod slow-ly, as if he were looking at something far in the dis-tance that was just coming into focus. "Yes, I think I see the sense of it," he conceded finally.

"Good, now let's get going," Casey said and started walking.

"Here." Theresa handed Arthur her heavy red bookbag.

"Pray, what's this?"

"A good start is carrying a girl's books."

"I feel I'm being made quite the fool," Arthur said to Casey as they walked a few feet behind Theresa.

"Probably," Casey nodded. "But you shouldn't worry about it too much. We've all had to do it."

16

hen they reached the Cobble Hill School, Arthur was immediately struck by all the commotion. Kids appeared from every street, and a line of big yellow busses discharged an endless stream of them as well. The school only held about four hundred students, but that was more than the entire number of people who lived in Arthur's small medieval village. Kids filled the area, more than Arthur had ever seen in his life. He stopped and looked up at the huge, majestic building of immaculate red brick and poured concrete.

"'Tis like a castle! This is all for you and your friends?"

"Relax Arthur, it's just a school."

"I'd expected a one room shack for a dozen children."

A small group of Theresa's friends were standing by the entrance, waiting to go in. They spotted her and one of them waved. "I gotta go," she said.

"I guess I'll see you guys at lunch. 'Bye Arthur."

"Farewell, M'lady," he said with a humble bow.

She started to walk off, her eyes on Arthur's as if she couldn't look away.

"Your books," Casey reminded her.

"Oh." She retreated and took them from Arthur's hands, still a victim of his powerful gaze. When she finally got free, her friends were eager to know who that was who'd been carrying her books. Casey watched her try to explain casually, but he could see them smile and glance in Arthur's direction a few times. They were too curious already. It's gonna be a long day, he thought.

Casey took Arthur into the administration office and registered him as his cousin and asked for a visitor's pass. When Mrs. Waters asked how long he'd be staying, Casey couldn't answer the question. He finally said that he wasn't sure, and it made him worry about just how long Arthur would be around and what would happen to him. The pass was issued for the week and would have to be renewed next Monday. It seemed like a year away. Casey realized that anything could happen to Arthur by then.

They left the office and went down the hall to Casey's homeroom. When Arthur spotted Mickey he became overjoyed, even though Casey had told him that he would be there.

"Mickey, my friend!"

"Hey Artie, how ya doin'. I didn't know you was gonna come to school with us."

"Yeah well, it just worked out that way," Casey explained.

"So you couldn't figure out—"

Casey knew what he was going to say and cut him off. "No, forget about that."

"Yeah, but—"

"I'll tell ya later, Mick."

Mickey looked from Casey to Arthur and nodded warily. "Okay, whatever."

"Take a seat, Arthur."

"And what of Kevin and Sean? I see them not."

"They're in a different homeroom. We'll see 'em later."

Arthur sat down and looked around the room. There were many pictures and drawings on the walls, as well as a large black slate at the front of the room. "Curious," he said to himself.

Then he noticed the desk and found that worthy of close examination, too.

Mickey's eyes were on Arthur the whole time. He couldn't wait for later. "Wow, the kid's still out of it. I can't believe it."

"Look, you gotta humor him. You gotta act like he is King Arthur."

"You're kiddin'."

"No, I'm real serious."

"You couldn't get anything outa him?"

"No. I was with him all yesterday. If he ain't King Arthur, then he sure oughta be."

Mickey shook his head. His eyes remained on Arthur, whose attention was now taken by the activities of all the other kids in the room as they prepared themselves for the day. He seemed fascinated by their books and pens and everything, and wished he had some of his own. "Maybe we shoulda just called the cops," Mickey said ominously.

"Well it's too late now."

"What're you gonna do with him?"

"I don't know," Casey conceded as he watched Arthur, who was sitting there as if he'd never seen a desk or a pencil or even a classroom.

After attendance was taken, it was time for Casey's first class. He led Arthur through the crowded hallways, in which a river of students rushed towards their classes as if they were already late.

"You endure this every day?" Arthur cried at the madness of the throng. "'Tis more urgent than a witch burning."

"Casey!" a loud voice called suddenly.

It was Cathy, his sister. She was behind them but he didn't turn or stop. Casey couldn't pretend that he hadn't heard her, but he was determined to ignore her anyway. When Arthur turned and saw her, his face lit up. "Ah, Cathy, you—"

Casey grabbed him immediately and dragged him off. "Come on, we'll be late for math." They had only a few minutes, but he didn't want to confront her. He knew there'd be questions to which he had no good answers.

The morning proceeded with no surprises. Casey told Arthur to look like he knew what was going on, and managed to keep him quiet after a few unavoidable introductions. Fortunately, Arthur was sufficiently mesmerized by the proceedings of each class to keep him out of trouble. Casey would tuck him into an empty seat at the back of each classroom and that would be the end of it.

He remained a little nervous, and would occasionally glance back to see how Arthur was doing. Wearing Casey's own jeans, sneakers and blue New York Giants sweatshirt, he looked surprisingly normal with a textbook in front of him, and actually appeared to be following the class. As long as he doesn't raise his hand, Casey thought, we'll be okay. He figured that if they could just get to lunchtime without incident, it would be smooth sailing the rest of the day. By then, enough people would know who Arthur was and the curiosity would subside.

"What now?" Arthur asked on the way to the last class of the afternoon.

"English."

"But you already speak english, almost as well as I."

"Yeah, but there's a lotta reading and writing. We're doing Shakespeare right now. It's hard as hell."

"Shakespeare?" Arthur repeated without a flicker of recognition. Casey had to admit that the kid was either the best actor in the world, or his condition really prevented him from acknowledging just about everything he'd ever learned.

As soon as the classroom was filled, Miss Newburg, the small spry english teacher stood up with her usual enthusiasm, her fat Complete Works of Shakespeare in her hand. She walked to the head of the class and plunged right in. "So, Henry V, the—" Then her gaze lit on Arthur. "Oh, we have a visitor. And who are you?"

"This is my cousin Arthur," Casey said for twentieth time that morning. "He's visiting for a while."

"Welcome, Arthur."

"Oh, thank you ma'am," Arthur responded happily.

Miss Newburg's expression changed suddenly. As effervescent as she was routinely, for she was also the drama teacher, she became even more animated at the sound of his distinct voice. "Oh, you're English!"

"Yes."

Casey should have seen it coming, but it was too late. And he probably wouldn't have been able to stop it anyway. All he could do was close his eyes and let it happen.

"Well, Shakespeare should be in your genes. We'd love to hear it read properly." Arthur had no idea what she was talking about, and Casey just sat there with a knot in his stomach, hoping for a fire drill or an earthquake. "Act IV, Scene 3, the famous St. Crispin's speech. Why don't you read it for us, Arthur. This should be a real treat, class." She stood there beaming, as if it were the happiest day of her life.

For a few seconds nothing happened, then Miss Newburg broke the silence. "Oh, you have no book. Casey, just give him yours and show him where to start."

Casey's movements were slow and deliberate. He could hardly breathe and his mouth was dry, but there was nothing he could do to save Arthur. This is it, he thought. We're doomed.

Arthur took the book, continuing to hold it open to the right place. Then he sat there and stared at the page, his expression subdued with fascination. Miss Newburg waited in rapt anticipation as the seconds ticked by.

After a minute or so, she cleared her throat and said, "Out loud Arthur, in your best stage voice. So we can all hear it."

Casey thought he was going to pass out. Aside from a few address numbers, he wasn't sure that Arthur could even read, and the entire classroom was waiting for him to recite an entire Shakespearean soliloquy! As the silence pressed down on him like the weight of the world, Casey forced himself to start coming up with excuses, although there were few that could credibly explain why a fourteen year-old boy from England couldn't read english.

That's when Arthur finally opened his mouth. He began to read the long, complex speech, unsure of himself at first. But he quickly found its rhythm, and somewhere around the middle, he found its meaning. Miss Newburg seemed happy, and nodded her head as Arthur's perfect British diction struck just the right notes in the nearly incomprehensible old language, transforming it into poetry. Even the rest of the class was able to make sense of it as they never had before, and was beginning to succumb to the exquisite pleasure of Shakespeare on their ears. Casey couldn't believe it, and he dared to imagine that they were actually going to make it to the end of class without exposure.

As Arthur neared the last third of the soliloquy, he stood up, moved by the marvelous language himself, and seemed to find the emotion in the scene. He didn't stumble or miss a word, casting an unbroken spell, even when he looked up momentarily and commented, "Say, this is quite good!" Arthur soon found his way to the head of the class, where Miss Newburg was standing, and performed the rest of the speech, transformed, not as if he were acting it, but living it. As if he were Henry addressing his troops one last time before they descended into battle, all those centuries ago.

'But we in it shall be remembered.
We few, we happy few, we band of brothers.
For he today that sheds his blood with me
Shall be my brother. Be he ne'er so vile,
This day shall gentle his condition.
And gentlemen in England now abed
Shall think themselves accurs'd they were not here,
And hold their manhoods cheap whiles any speaks
That fought us upon Saint Crispin's day.'

When he'd uttered those famous, resonant words, "We happy few, we... band of brothers," Arthur seemed to be on the verge of tears. He felt the words and their terrible meaning deep down, for they were completely real to him. If Casey didn't know better, assuming that he did know better, he'd swear that Arthur was just learning them for the first time. They were not old, clumsy verses that no longer made sense. They'd tripped off his tongue as if no one had ever said them before, as if he'd invented them himself, in the heat of the moment. Indeed, to Arthur's medieval mind, Shakespeare was still four hundred years away, and he was moved only as a future king could be moved by such noble sentiment.

When he stopped there was silence again, but of a very different nature. The class was too stunned to even applaud. Miss Newburg wiped her eyes and said, "Arthur, that was beautiful. It was just the most magnificent... " Then she exhaled, slightly overcome once again.

Arthur sat down again and returned the book to Casey. "That was amazing, Arthur."

"For the first time, I think I know what it really means to be a king," Arthur admitted, still a bit stunned. "I should like to learn the rest of that story."

"I can't believe it," Casey whispered as Miss Newburg proceeded to resume the class. "Why'd you take so long to start?"

"I had to read it once through to gain its meaning."

"I didn't even know if you could read that good."

"Oh yes. When I and my fellows were particularly troublesome, the village friar made us read aloud from the Bible until we begged to be let go."

When lunchtime rolled around, Casey was brimming with a rare confidence. He was sure that the worst was behind them, no matter what Arthur did now. They met up with Kevin and Sean again in the cafeteria, and it was a joyful reunion. He called them my new Irish mates and they happily referred to him as their limey pal, and all laughed as if they were old friends. Unfortunately, the scene attracted too much attention, and Cathy was finally able to corner her little brother.

"Okay squirt, what's going on?"

"What d'you mean?"

"I know you Casey, something's up." They all looked at him and clammed up. Cathy read their strained expressions and then looked at Arthur for a moment. "It's him, isn't it? He's not really from England, right?"

Sean snickered and put his hands over his mouth. Kevin punched him and whispered, "Shut up."

"No, he's really from England," Casey explained coolly.

She looked at Arthur closely, as if waiting for him to slip up.

"Yes, you have my word as a king," he assured Cathy, locking eyes with her until she looked away.

"What, you're from an especially honest family or something?"

"Leave him alone, Cath, huh."

"Yeah, what's your problem?" Mickey added. "The guy's new in school and we're just tryin' to be nice to him."

"I've never seen you guys be this nice to anyone in my whole life."

"I guess we're finally growin' up," Casey said firmly. He knew they'd held her off, for the moment.

"Well, isn't this cozy!" It was Frank Mayo, not missing another opportunity to be obnoxious. He looked Arthur up and down. "Where's your costume? I almost didn't recognize you." Seeing Arthur in contemporary clothing and without his sword had apparently restored Frank's confidence.

"Funny, Frank," Casey said quickly, hoping Cathy would miss the reference.

"You must gotta lotta time on your hands, Cath, f'you gotta hang around these mooks." Frank leaned in towards her, trying to be tough. The leer on his stupid face was impossible to ignore. "G'out with me and I'll keep ya busy."

"I don't like your manner, sir," Arthur said pointedly, and glared up at Frank from his seat.

"Uh-oh," Mickey muttered.

"What?" Frank looked at Arthur, incredulous.

"You should stand down and ask her pardon. This maid is too fair for your coarse advances."

"Hey," he said with a grin, "I'll bet she's better than fair!"

If he'd had his sword, Arthur would surely have cut off Frank's empty head while the vile smirk still hung from his mug. But all he could do instead was grab Frank ignobly by his bottom lip, which Arthur used to pull him down to his eye-level. Frank slurred and waved his arms in protest.

"Jeez Arthur," Casey cried. "Whadaya doing?"

"This wretch knows none of the behavior that Theresa assured me was proper. This is your sister and no one can speak to her that way."

Kevin and Sean couldn't believe their eyes, and Cathy was also stunned by the whole exchange. She had to remind herself that all this was on her behalf. "Wow," was her only response.

When others began to notice and heads turned, Casey started to panic. "Come on, let him go," he pleaded.

"With no apology?!"

Although red-faced and drooling, Frank grabbed Arthur's wrist in a desperate attempt to defend himself. But he couldn't free his precious lip from Arthur's thumb and forefinger. It looked as if Arthur was about to tear it off.

"Arthur!" It was Casey's expression that finally saved him.

Arthur couldn't help notice that he appeared to be going out of his mind, so he simply let go.

Frank's hands went right to his face and covered his sore mouth. "You are dead after school!" he slobbered madly. "Hear me, dead!" Then he stalked out of the cafeteria, still holding his damaged lip.

"That was incredible," Mickey commented. "I gotta remember that move."

Casey put his head in his hands. "Great Arthur! Just great! We were home free and you get into a fight with Frank Mayo!"

"T'was no fault of mine."

"Yeah, Case," Kevin said pointlessly. "He started it."

Casey stared at the table. How'm I gonna get him outa this one? he thought.

"Maybe we should just call the cops," Sean suggested.

17

asey spent the rest of the day worrying about Frank Mayo. He'd hoped that Frank would forget the whole thing, for he was always threatening to kill somebody after school and nothing ever happened. But this time was different. With so many witnesses in the cafeteria and everybody wondering who Arthur was, news and anticipation of the fight escalated with each passing hour. Yet again, Arthur's plight was determined by the great rumor mill.

Frank was particularly swept up in the furor. Every time classes let out and the halls teemed with students, there were a few more jerks happy to cheer Frank on. Even those who hadn't witnessed the altercation in the cafeteria were ready to see Frank "finish off this mook," as he put it. To make things worse, some of the older kids had cell phones, and were quick to instant message the latest developments all over the school. When Frank passed Casey and Arthur in the hallway after fifth period, he even made a big show of pointing at Arthur and making a fist. Bystanders expected a fight right there. This wouldn't have been so bad, Casey realized. Mr. Kraft, the history teacher and ex-Marine, or one of the gym teachers, probably would've been on them in seconds and broken it up. This might've satisfied Frank. But with the big stand-off, he wasn't going to forget about this one. Frank couldn't just let "some new kid" challenge his reputation.

Casey was totally frazzled by eighth period, the last one of the day. He knew that a confrontation couldn't be avoided, and there was no one he could call to stop it, without risking having to explain about Arthur. He truly wished that they *had* called the cops yesterday, which now seemed like years ago. Despite Arthur's casual fearlessness on his sister's behalf, Casey imagined that he was totally unprepared for a real fight and the brutal reality of it would traumatize him for life. If it made him recall terrible memories of life at home, Arthur might end up unable to talk or move forever. Casey remembered more of his aunt's ominous words. An un... communicative state, she'd called it. A shell. The hopelessness of those terms was overwhelming, and sent hot fear surging through him.

When Casey nervously packed up his books at the end of the period, he and Arthur left history class and went back to his homeroom. He could hear whispers and feel eyes on them the whole way. There were fifteen more minutes before school let out for the day.

Casey stared at the clock as afternoon attendance was taken.

"This is it, Arthur. I don't know what we're gonna
do."

"Did I not say just yesterday that mercy only
prolongs such confrontations? I should have
relieved the impertinent rogue of his head when I
had the chance."

Casey said nothing. He just sat there wondering how his life had changed so completely in a
single day.

Arthur noticed his hopeless manner and placed
a firm hand on his shoulder. "Fear not, my friend.
This wretch is no match for me. What kind of
king—"

"Arthur!" Casey insisted. "Frank's bigger and
older and a lot meaner than you. All he can do is
fight. And believe me, he's gonna be lookin' forward to this one. Along with the rest of the
school."

"There shall be no fight, Casey. For I mean to
jump him on the road, before our place of meeting,
and dispatch him there."

"What? You can't do that. He'll just wanna
fight you again later."

"But he shall be dead," Arthur announced with
a laugh.

"You can't kill him."

"But he means to kill me. 'Dead after school'
were his exact words, I recall."

Casey shook his head and groaned. The misunderstanding was almost funny. "That's just an expression, an exaggeration. He's not gonna actually kill you, just beat you up. Then the fight's over and that's then end of it. Get it?"

"Hm. I don't know if I accept those conditions. It's so much easier just to kill somebody. The matter is more permanently concluded, then."

"If you kill him you'll be arrested and sent to jail."

"Then what must I do instead?"

"You've gotta fight him, with your hands." Casey put up his fists to demonstrate.

"You mean wrestle?" Casey nodded. "T'will be a Greco-Roman match then?"

"No, there's no rules."

"Then I can kill him."

"No!"

Now Arthur groaned with frustration. "If there's no rules, then I ought to take him by surprise, like any sworn enemy! I'd also opt for a full confrontation between his forces and mine on the field of battle."

"It's gotta be a fair fight," Casey said emphatically. "Just between the two of you. Then when it's over and one of you gives up, that's it."

"And neither of us are dead."

"Right. You can even shake hands and be friends after that."

"And we are enemies no longer." Arthur looked away dreamily and thought for a moment. "Curious, but I see the sense of it. The matter is concluded by mutual agreement that we don't have to hate each other. We can even be allies in the face of another enemy." He nodded. "Yes... " The notion seemed to carry Arthur off, as if it were something that he'd never considered before. A smile crept across his innocent face.

"What?" Casey asked when he noticed his expression.

"'Tis a fair gambit, then. Based on simple respect between men."

Arthur knew nothing of boxing or fist fighting. Since everyone back home carried a sword or dagger, fights resulted in quick bloodshed. The notion of striking someone with a hand instead of a weapon seemed bizarre to Arthur, and Casey had to demonstrate the act of punching to him. Although Arthur had had his share of childhood tussles with other boys, they'd always consisted of kicking, scratching, gouging, finger-poking and hair-pulling. Casey explained that all this was unfair and cowardly. Indeed, only girls fought this way, and such tactics were sadly ineffective against someone who was ready to pound you senseless with his fists.

Arthur understood and was ready to put up his dukes, like Casey showed him. But his complete unfamiliarity with this form of fighting made him awkward and uncoordinated. He looked like a girl anyway, and Casey could see that Arthur was going to have the hell beat out of him no matter what he taught him.

"I'm gonna tell Frank to leave you alone," Cathy said as they all stood outside the school's front entrance. "I won't let anyone fight over me."

"They're not fighting *over* you," Casey reminded her. "They're fighting because of you. If you weren't so damn nosy—"

"Me?!"

"Frank could use a good beating," Mickey said, balling up his fist and striking his palm. "If somebody would just—"

"You could always go out with him," Kevin suggested half-seriously.

"It's a bit late for that," Cathy said. "Besides, I don't wanna go out with him and he knows I never will."

"So what're we gonna do?" Mickey asked. "We can't let him just bash Artie's head in."

They were supposed to meet Frank up the street and around the corner in an empty lot. Just about every school fight took place there, for the lot was close enough to the school to prevent cooling off or chickening out, but too far away for any faculty or administrators to pass by and stop the show.

"We better get going," Casey said finally. "I'll bet Frank's already there."

"Why don't you just not show up," Cathy suggested.

"And hafta go through this again until we do? No way."

"Yeah," Kevin said. "Ya gotta stand up. Artie's just gonna hafta get it over with."

Cathy put a gentle hand on his arm. "I'm sorry, Arthur. I can't help feeling a little responsible for all this."

"Think nothing of it, fair one. I'm only too glad to thrash this malcontent for the good of all."

Casey shook his head. Hopeless, he thought.

The small crowd made its way to the lot, followed by a much bigger and more enthusiastic one of spectators. Although nobody seemed to have much affection for Frank Mayo, more than a few in the crowd couldn't help but appraise the event in his favor.

"You're gonna get your ass kicked, pal."

"Yeah, I'm sure glad I'm not you."

"Maybe if you just take a few good shots and lay down he'll go easy on you."

"I've never seen Frank this mad."

"I heard you sucker punched him in the lunchroom. That was pretty stupid, man."

"Yeah, you really asked for it."

Casey didn't say anything, but he would have liked to bust all their heads in at the moment. If it hadn't been for all the talk about what had happened in the cafeteria, there wouldn't be any fight now. Nobody even liked Frank that much. Everyone was just swept up in the excitement and wanted to get in on the big event. Casey was afraid to even look at Arthur. But when he finally glanced at him just before they reached the lot, Casey saw a grimness in his face that he'd never seen on someone his own age. It was an expression that he'd only seen on those of soldiers in books about war. It was the face of someone going into battle.

The lot was bordered by a corrugated metal fence that only covered half the opening. The ground was hard-packed dirt dotted with clumps of weeds and strewn with rocks and odd debris. Aside from the usual broken bottles, there was a broken chair, an old broom handle, a few bricks and two-by-fours, a pool cue, an umbrella, and an old stove with no door. Frank Mayo was leaning on the stove, flanked by a couple of equally useless friends smoking cigarettes and a few members of the varsity football team.

He clapped his hands when the crowd appeared at the mouth of the lot. "'Bout time," he said. "I thought you rabbited and I'd hafta go lookin' for ya."

"We all should just take him out," Mickey muttered.

"Yeah, he wouldn't go after all of us," Kevin said.

Casey wished for such a miracle. Getting beat up in front of the whole school would keep Frank out of sight for the rest of the year. But he and his friends stayed timidly on the sidewalk with the rest of the crowd. Doom was already in the air. Frank had taken further control of the situation by seizing the lot as if it were his territory. Casey never felt so bad in his life. It was as if he were just sacrificing his confused, helpless friend for his own safety. He could hear himself saying, Sorry Arthur, you just gotta fight him. That's the way things are.

Frank stepped forward and pounded his fist into his hand. "Let's go. You take a good beating and it'll be over quick."

"Why d'you hafta be such a jerk, Frank!" Cathy shouted.

"What, you're gonna love me forever if I call it off?"

"It'd be a start," Mickey drawled.

"I wish you could just shut him up for good, Arthur," she spat.

Arthur hadn't heard the last few exchanges. He'd fixed his intense gaze on Frank's face the moment he saw him and had yet to blink or look away. He hadn't moved, even to push the hair out of his eyes to get a clear view of his foe. Everybody looked from Frank to Arthur, to see what he was going to do now that the time had finally come.

Theresa was standing a few feet back in the crowd. She felt like she had to do something before it was too late. She didn't know quite why, but she had to make contact with Arthur, if only briefly. She stepped forward and slipped in next to him. "Wait, Arthur," she said softly. "You won't be able to see."

"Hey, what is this?!" Frank protested.

"He's stallin'," a football player called out.

"Whadaya 'spect," said one of Frank's two cronies.

Arthur barely noticed Theresa as she took off her red scarf and tied it around his head to hold back his messy blond bangs. She touched his arm when she finished and said, "Okay. Please don't get hurt."

Arthur didn't turn his head or look at her, but just stepped forward. The grim, intense countenance never altered, and the clear blue eyes never wavered from the face of his enemy. Neither Casey, nor anyone else there could have known the Arthur they now saw before them. Despite his contemporary blue jeans and his borrowed sweatshirt, Arthur was still from another time. The modern disguise could not prevent him from being a medieval boy, especially one who happened to be a king. Even Frank Mayo, who'd had his share of fights and wasn't afraid of anyone, was still only a dumb high school kid whose life had never truly been threatened.

For Arthur, fighting meant only for one's life.

"Here he comes, Frank!" warned one of his friends.

Frank was slightly startled by the sight of Arthur coming straight at him, his face stern and unafraid. Arthur started to raise his hands, but when he was a few feet away, Frank stepped forward quickly and punched him right in the face. The crowd gasped as one and Casey called out "No!" and bit his lip.

Arthur was spun half around by the strange action. But his face was unchanged. He turned and closed in again, and Frank immediately struck him with his other hand. Arthur doubled over and remained there for a moment. Casey wished that he would just go down so Frank would be satisfied. But Arthur looked up and suddenly ran at Frank without warning. He barreled into him and they plowed into the small group standing by the old stove, scattering them. Frank let out a yelp as he hit the stove and the two of them rolled off it onto the hard ground.

"Get him, Artie!" Kevin yelled.

With Frank beneath him, Arthur locked his hands together and pounded away at Frank as if he were unaware of what he was doing. Arthur's face maintained its grim composure, but he kept bludgeoning Frank as if his coupled hands were a club. The medieval warrior was completely free of the lost, innocent young boy. He sought to vanquish his foe as if his life, honor and position were at stake. The crowd was stunned by his brutality. Even Casey hoped that he would stop.

But Frank still had his size and weight to his advantage. Arthur would have pounded him unconscious, but Frank bucked him off him and stood up, more enraged than ever. Cursing and screaming, he began kicking Arthur uncontrollably. But Frank couldn't prevent him from getting his hands on the broken pool cue laying by his head.

No one could see just how Arthur had seen it or was able to pick it up, for it just seemed to be in his grip and in the same motion lodged between Frank's legs, tripping him. Arthur jumped to his feet, holding the pool cue like a weapon of his own time, the quarter-staff. He brandished it defensively, waiting for Frank to get up.

Arthur's face was bloody and bruised, and his lip noticeably swollen. But he showed his teeth, almost smiling. His determination was frightening as he stepped forward to roundhouse Frank on the side of his head with the fat end of the cue. Frank spun around and Arthur poked him hard with the end of the stick in the stomach, bending him in over.

"Hey, no fair!" someone shouted.

"Yeah!" echoed one of the football players. Arthur noticed the crowd and the faces of Frank's supporters, and something changed in his face.

He looked at Frank again with an awareness of a new component in the contest. He stepped away, to where the broom handle was lying, and sent it towards Frank with a flick of the end of the pool cue.

"Fair fight, then," Arthur called. The broom handle bounced at Frank's feet and came to a stop. Frank was still dazed and was slow to act. He just looked at the fat stick before him. "Pick it up!" Arthur ordered.

Frank held it up, not sure how to use it. But his hands moved to one end and he started swinging it at Arthur like a baseball bat. He seemed to like the motion and was suddenly himself again, going at Arthur with the clear intent of mercilessly cracking him over the head.

"Yeah, Frank, now you got him!"

"Watch out Arthur!"

It indeed looked like Arthur was now in trouble, for the broom handle was longer than the pool cue and Frank was taller and had a longer reach. But Arthur parried the swings skillfully, frustrating Frank and causing him to become over-eager and sloppy. Frank continued to swing the broom handle wildly, grunting with each attempt. Then Arthur made his move. With a quick lunge and twist of the cue, he yanked the broom handle out of Frank's hands and forced him back with flat blows to the chest. Frank stumbled backwards over the broken chair and knocked the wind out of himself. Gasping, Frank was helpless when Arthur stood over him with the end of the pool cue

to his throat. Arthur relented only when he finally heard Casey's frantic protests.

"He's choking! Let him go!"

Arthur tossed the pool cue aside and stepped
back. The grimness left him and he looked like
any fourteen year-old boy in the crowd. "The contest is ended," Arthur said clearly. "We can be
friends now."

"What?" Frank managed to say through his
strained breaths.

"Friends. We are friends, as is the custom
here." He grabbed Frank's hand and pulled him
up into a sitting position, then shook it heartily.

"Uh... " Frank put his hand to his sore chest
when Arthur let go.

"Now we are better men, not because we fought,
but because we chose not to in the end. 'Tis a better, more noble conclusion than a pointless battle
to the death."

"Yeah, sure. For now anyway."

Arthur turned and walked back towards the
crowd, which parted to let him by.

"Jeez Arthur, you beat the hell out of him!"
Kevin cried, slapping him on the back.

"No, we both fought well, with fury and honor.
That I bested him is without importance."

"Yeah, but it's still pretty cool."

Theresa put her hand to his swollen lip. "This
looks bad. Does it hurt, Arthur?"

Arthur looked at her and then realized that
there was something on his head. He ran his fingers through his hair and came away with her red

scarf.

"I can take that back if you want." Demurely, she took it from him.

"T'was for good fortune in battle. I thank you."

She smiled warmly, unable to free herself from his marvelous gaze.

"He should go home," Cathy instructed. "He's gotta put some ice on that."

"Yeah," Casey agreed, starting to worry again.

18

fter they were finally free of the jubilant crowd, Casey suggested that Arthur come back to his house to fix himself up. He said it casually, but only for Cathy's benefit. Since Arthur still had nowhere to go, he just couldn't go home and clean up like anyone else. But Casey didn't want Cathy to get suspicious again, so he added that it would be better if Arthur came over to their house to prevent his mom from finding out that he'd been in a fight. Cathy didn't even respond to the matter, and Casey felt that the situation was covered for at least the next few hours. But he seriously doubted that he could keep Arthur there throughout dinner again and be able to sneak him upstairs for the night.

"What're you guys doing later?" Casey asked self-consciously when they reached the corner of Carroll Street.

"Um, nothing, I guess," Kevin said.

"Yeah, you know, dinner, homework, the usual," Mickey added.

"Well, uh," Casey began, looking at Mickey, "we may stop by when I walk Arthur home," he said for his sister's benefit. "I told him about your Playstation and he really wants to see it." There was urgency in his eyes as he tried to convey his real message secretly.

Mickey wasn't sure what he was getting at, but he still took the hint. "Yeah, sure. Just call first."

"Why d'you need to walk Arthur home?" Cathy asked suddenly.

Casey felt hot fear surge through him. "Um, he's still a little confused about the neighborhood. The streets and stuff. I also like to point out stuff while we're walking." Cathy's face didn't reveal anything, but Casey was afraid that he'd said too much. She was hard to fool for long.

"Hey, I think Theresa likes you, Arthur," Kevin said with a smirk. Sean just giggled.

"The light's red," Cathy announced and started to walk away.

"Yeah, okay. See ya tomorrow, Case."

"Right" he whispered. "Listen, I gotta find Arthur a place to stay tonight. I can't risk another one in my house. Cathy's gonna catch on soon."

"Don't look at us," Kevin implored. "Our place is jammed, with my little sister and my gran'mother and all."

"Yeah," Sean added. "Someone'll find him for sure and call the cops."

"Then he'll hafta stay at mine," Mickey decided.

"Tony's away at school, so he can always use his room."

"Good, I was hoping you'd say that," Casey said, relieved.

"I'm just not sure how we're gonna get him up there. Come over later and we'll see what we can do."

Casey nodded. "Okay."

"Come on!" Cathy called from halfway up the block. "He's gotta put ice on that lip!"

They took Arthur home and cleaned him up. Casey gave him another sweatshirt and wrapped a few ice cubes in a dish towel for him to hold against his lip. When Casey's parents got home, they were a little surprised to find Arthur in the kitchen with a swollen lip and a bruised face. Casey quickly explained the situation, and his mother was ready to call Arthur's house to tell his mother that everything was all right. Casey was able to distract her with the news that Arthur had fought Frank Mayo for Cathy's honor. This revelation made Casey's parents completely forget their previous interest in being neighborly. They were too busy being amazed and baffled.

"We should be thankful for Arthur's chivalry, but I'd figured we were free of that idiot," Casey's father said.

"My what?" Arthur wondered.

Casey's mother shook her head. "I'm so sorry, Arthur. This isn't the kind of thing that you should have to face at a new school. I'm just so embarrassed." She kept shaking her head.

"I sure hope this isn't going to be an on-going

problem," his father added, looking at Cathy the whole time.

"What are you looking at me for?" she protested. "It wasn't my fault."

"Yeah," Casey agreed. "He was looking for trouble and Arthur just got in the way."

"I think he took a disliking to me that first day, on the way here from the park," Arthur said.

"You didn't tell me about that," Cathy said. "I knew there was something going on around here."

"Don't worry about it," Casey said, hoping that Cathy would now be satisfied. "I'll make sure Arthur stays away from Frank for a while."

"Well after that beating I doubt he'll show his face again," she gloated.

"Cathy," her mother scolded.

Casey's father glanced at his watch. "Why don't we drive Arthur home," he suggested. Casey went white. "Come on Case, you're gonna miss that old car after this week."

"Uh, yeah, but I promised Arthur we'd go over to Mickey's on the way home, so we might as well walk."

"Have it your way. But maybe Arthur would like to come with us when we pick up the new one on Saturday."

"Yeah, sure." Casey looked directly at Arthur. "Your lip looks okay, so we should get going."

"Since you're showing Arthur around," Casey's mother began, "you can go to the post office. I need something mailed certified."

There was no way out of it, so Casey just tried

to agree happily. "Sure, Mom."

Casey got Arthur out of there as quickly as possible. It was just too risky with his parents hanging over them, being overly friendly and hospitable. Casey also concluded that no matter how Arthur dressed or acted, something about him just made him stand out. Sitting there in the kitchen, trying to look like any other troubled teenager, Arthur was as obvious and unnatural as he'd ever been.

"Mickey should have things figured out by now," Casey said on the way back down Garfield. "I'll stay a while then go home for dinner. But I'll see you at school tomorrow, Arthur."

He nodded responsively. But his thoughts seemed to be somewhere else. It looked as if Arthur had lost all his previous curiosity, and was no longer interested in his new surroundings.

"I've become a problem for you and your friends," he admitted sadly.

Casey was surprised by the statement, but he felt Arthur's discomfort. "No, not really. It's been fun having you around."

Arthur looked away. "But you've been wondering what shall become of me. And I, too."

"I guess. But don't worry about it, okay? We'll... figure things out soon."

Surprisingly, Arthur smiled. Casey couldn't recall seeing him do it before. "If Merlin were here, he'd announce that we shouldn't just wait for fate to find us and off we'd go."

"To do what?"

"To find... a sign, a vision, something with

meaning to give us direction." He sounded wistful, as if he actually missed Merlin's crazy excursions all over the medieval countryside.

"I wouldn't know a sign if it was right in front of me," Casey said, then wished he hadn't. But he had no idea what Arthur was really looking for, or if he even knew himself.

Mickey lived in Carroll Gardens, not far from Casey, in the next neighborhood over. The route would be familiar to Arthur, for it was in the same direction as school. But the big post office was about ten blocks away, on Fulton Street and Flatbush Avenue, which cut straight through the heart of Brooklyn. They walked down 5th until the avenue suddenly opened up onto a double-wide, two-way thoroughfare. Despite what he'd seen up to then, Arthur was unprepared for the level of noise and activity on Flatbush. He didn't know which way to look first. They hurried across and went up the wide stairs to the huge post office, which Arthur found nearly as impressive as the Duke's castle. He marveled at the spectacle of so many people mailing and receiving envelopes and packages of every size and color, forcing Casey to explain what might be inside them all. Including Arthur's distraction, they were back out on the street in ten minutes. When they reached the corner of 4th, they had to stop and wait for the light to change. It would be the second time they'd crossed Flatbush in the last half hour. Casey hadn't identified any of the streets to Arthur, because he believed he knew them all in the back of his mind.

When the light turned green and they approached the other side of the street, Arthur happened to look up. What he saw on the sign above made him stop immediately. "What's that?" he asked, pointing at it like a small child.

"A lamppost."

"Those letters," Arthur said wondrously. "They read... Flatbush."

"That's just a street sign, Arthur. This is Flatbush Avenue. It's the same big street we crossed just before."

Arthur's expression changed from cautious to euphoric. He now looked like he did when he'd pulled the sword from the stone. "This is it," he said softly. "This is why I'm here." Then he fell to his knees and embraced the lamppost desperately.

"Arthur?" Casey had stopped and turned around. He didn't know what to think now. Despite all the trouble Arthur had been, Casey was somewhat used to him. His behavior was consistent and he was actually becoming predictable. Casey wasn't that worried about him, even if he still believed that there must be something fundamentally wrong with him. But all his worst fears came rushing back at the sight of Arthur on his knees with his arms around the lamppost. "Come on Arthur, what is it?"

He rose and stepped forward. He looked Casey in the eye and said, with both assurance and wonder, "I've been sent here for a reason."

"Why?" Casey was enthralled and couldn't wait for his answer.

"I'm not sure. But my journey must be a... a

quest for something. T'was the Duke of Flatbush that ordered my banishment. It can be no coincidence that I ended up here, when he could have sent me anywhere. Or better yet, killed me."

"The Duke of Flatbush?"

"Yes. I tried to gain his support, so the people would accept me as King. But he would not be swayed." Arthur extended his arms as wide as he could. "So this is my punishment."

A strange feeling crept over Casey as he looked into Arthur's face. Then a thought entered his head as if sent from somewhere else. He's not crazy or confused. Suddenly, Arthur seemed completely different than he had a few moments before. Casey was aware of what he was really telling himself, but he made no attempt to talk himself out of it. Instead, he had another idea.

"Arthur, tell me everything about how you got here."

"Everything?"

"Yes. Everything that led up to it, going as far back as you can."

19

rthur told Casey the entire story, from before he met Merlin to the moment he tried to re-enter the Duke's castle. Because Arthur was from a time before television and movies and radio, and even the printed word, the only form of mass communication was verbal storytelling. This meant that Arthur left nothing out. He accounted for every detail of his young life over the last month. The story took more time than the walk to Mickey's, and Arthur continued his colorful tale up in Mickey's room, barely pausing to say hello.

He was impressed when Mickey's black German shepherd, Rocky, showed up near the end of his account. The dog caused Arthur to comment that Mickey's family must be very rich. Casey and Mickey were confused by this, and Arthur explained that only the wealthy owned dogs and horses back home.

"He's just one dog." Mickey scratched Rocky's

head, still a bit perplexed. "We've had him for years."

"Is that it?" Casey asked, eager for more of Arthur's biography.

"Yes, nearly. I should add that Merlin was wrong again. I realize now that the flash of light he saw in his vision was from Melora, and not the sunlight in the highest window in the castle. I wonder if he even knows where I am, or if he was sent somewhere himself."

"You don't think ol' Merlin's wandering around Brooklyn right now, do ya?" Mickey asked.

Casey didn't know if Mickey was being serious, but both he and Arthur couldn't help taking the question that way.

Arthur looked worried for a moment, thinking the matter over. "No," he decided, shaking his head. "He'd have found me by now. And the best punishment for Merlin would be for the Duke to explain what happened to me and then leave Merlin to suffer his own magic trying to get me back."

"I thought Merlin could do anything," Mickey said.

"He's just getting started," Casey explained, Mickey having missed that part of the story. "He's not a real wizard yet."

"Oh."

"Now, if I can determine just why I'm here, I shall be able to find my way home."

"Well let's hope it's as obvious as Flatbush Avenue," Casey said. "We'll just have to think about it until we figure it out."

"Uh, yeah," Mickey pretended to agree. He'd been watching Casey since he and Arthur had arrived. It was apparent that Casey's opinion of Arthur had changed completely. He now seemed to take Arthur at his word. It's impossible, Mickey thought. He thinks he's really King Arthur!

Mickey couldn't say anything to Casey about it. He didn't know how to raise the matter while Arthur was present, and then Casey had to leave. He only stayed long enough for he and Mickey to show Arthur around the house and figure out a way for him to stay overnight in Mickey's brother's bedroom. They decided to be smart about the whole thing by not being secretive. Mickey would tell his parents that Arthur was new in school and had just moved to Brooklyn. But their house still wasn't ready and his parents were staying at a hotel until it was done. Mickey counted on his mother telling Arthur that he could stay with them as long as he liked, since they had an extra bedroom. This worked as planned, and Arthur moved into Tony's room without the least resistance or suspicion. Tony had even left some clothes that he'd grown out of, most of which fit Arthur perfectly.

When Casey left, he was a little relieved to be free of Arthur for a while. But his intentions were entirely unselfish. He was eager to go over Arthur's situation by himself, as seriously as he could, and maybe even come up with a solution. Walking home, he felt almost prickly with anticipation. He was forced to accept that Arthur's situation could only be fully explained if he were exactly who he said he was. Casey was almost relieved to realize that there was no other alternative.

When Casey got home he had just enough time to wash up and come down for dinner. As soon as he stepped into the kitchen he stopped in his tracks. It was the sight of the wet rag they'd filled with ice and used on Arthur's swollen lip that produced the sudden reaction.

His mother looked up and was distracted by her son's intense expression. "Casey, are you all right?"

"Huh? Oh, yeah," he responded, finding himself again. "I just remembered something."

"Where's Arthur?" Cathy asked without suspicion.

He almost hesitated. "Home, where else?"

"I don't know."

"Miss him already, huh?"

"I still can't believe what he did in the cafeteria today. Why'd he do that?"

"You're asking why he defended your honor?" their mother asked, half seriously.

"No, Mom, it was the way he did it. He's not like other boys, he's... I can't explain it. You just had to be there."

She turned towards her brother. "You know what I mean, right?"

He considered shrugging it off or denying it. But he just nodded casually after a moment. "Yeah, I do. Dad, can I use the computer after dinner?"

"Okay, but you better not be fooling around on the net."

"I have to look something up. Just for an hour."

Casey couldn't wait to get into his father's office after dinner. He turned on the computer and went right to the New York Public Library Research Site. Within seconds he was scanning through endless pages of medieval British history and mythology.

He figured that all he had to do was find references to the Duke of Flatbush and everything would start to make sense.

But there was no Duke. The only Flatbush Casey could find was an old family that went back to the 1600s. There was nothing called Flatbush before that. There was no shortage of information about King Arthur, however, and Casey could barely navigate it all. He'd hoped for some minor, but easily identifiable, story containing the two that would allow him to place Arthur's journey in context. Then Casey discovered something that really worried him. He tried to find information about Arthur's teenage years, and found out that there wasn't supposed to be a real King Arthur at all. He was a fictional character, alive only in stories and folklore that spanned five centuries. Although he was probably based on a real king, it couldn't be determined who that had been or even when he'd lived.

Casey was lost and disappointed. Then he remembered his revelation in the kitchen. Looking at the wet rag, he'd realized that Arthur hadn't ever heard the word *chivalry*. Casey's father had thanked him for his chivalry, upon which Arthur had said only, My what? Suddenly, Casey fully understood why none of Arthur's early years as King would be there among the hundreds of pages in front of him. What's more, he knew that neither the greatest scholars nor the most thorough books in all the libraries in the world could shed any light on Arthur's adolescence.

If it had always been assumed that Arthur never existed, then his legend would never account for a real childhood. This information was useless, for Arthur's mythology needed only his most important exploits. Arthur's life as a hero and symbol had begun when he pulled the sword from the stone. But if he'd been a real boy and no one knew about it, his real childhood would have been completely ignored. And now, so many hundreds of years later, it would no longer exist officially.

Arthur didn't know of chivalry or any of the other aspects of his own legend, because they had yet to be conceived. None of them could have existed already intact. They had to have been thought of and then subjected to their own evolution, like any real system of laws or beliefs. And these notions would most likely have occurred during Arthur's adolescence, as a result of Arthur's own thoughts and experiences. Casey seized on this notion. Nobody, no matter how good an actor or how much he knew of the legend, would ever have reacted to Mickey's dog the way that Arthur had. Or assumed that he'd have to fight Frank Mayo to the death. If he were just some disturbed kid pretending to be King Arthur, he'd have spouted all the known references to the established hero. He'd have acted the familiar part, like any kid on

Halloween. He'd have known of chivalry and valor and all the rest of it! But Arthur, Casey now knew for sure, was not just pretending. He couldn't pretend to be King Arthur, for he *was* King Arthur.

But what of Arthur's journey to the present? With no more references to the Duke of Flatbush, Casey couldn't get any closer to an answer or a solution. He scanned the pages back and forth, until he ran out of hope and patience. The lack of information that verified Arthur's existence as a real boy, also seemed to seal his fate in this strange time and place. If Arthur had indeed been sent on a quest, the reason was still incomprehensible. Casey had desperately wanted to be able to explain everything to his friend when he saw him the next day. But he would be forced to tell Arthur that he would have to figure out the means of his return by himself, for the last thousand years of history, mythology and literature offered not a single clue.

20

In the meantime, Arthur had a great time at Mickey's house. To his surprise, his family was much different than Casey's. They were louder and much more lively in their talk and behavior, especially over dinner. Arthur was immediately reminded of home.

They had a most enjoyable and interesting food that Arthur had never even heard of, spaghetti and meatballs. Arthur had three helpings, which endeared him to Mickey's mother right away.

There was boisterous and animated conversation between Mickey's parents, which took their attention away from Arthur. He was fascinated by their great physical presence. They seemed to fill the room to the walls. This was mostly due to the way they talked, waving their hands to emphasize their words, which were inflected with a harsh but colorful accent.

"So whadaya gonna do, Sal? He's determined to be at the head of the table, and he won't take no for an answer. I talked to him today and he mentioned it again, and it's only September."

"Don't worry Marie, I got it all figured out," he assured her with a wink and his finger in the air.

"IIow?" She put her hands on her hips. "Now that your father's gone, someone's gotta take his place. He expects it."

Mickey explained to Arthur that they were talking about Thanksgiving dinner, and who would take his grandfather's place at the head of the table, where he'd sat for almost fifty years. Arthur understood the matter completely, for it was an honor not to be bestowed without consideration.

"I'm gonna beat him at his own game," Mickey's father said with a grin.

"He's older than you, and he's not gonna care that this is your house. You take this away from him and we'll never hear the end if it."

Mickey's father waved his finger as if pointing at the ceiling. "My grandmother's old table in the attic. I'm gonna take it down and refinish it."

His wife threw up her hands. "So?"

"When all the flaps are up, Marie, it's *round*. There's no head for Mario to sit at."

"Then there's none for you, neither."

"I don't care, he does! But he won't be able to argue with grandma's old table. There's no head, everybody'll be equal, and he'll just hafta shut up."

Arthur had listened with interest, and now he finally spoke up. "So you concede the head of the table in your own house, for the unity and goodness of all, sir?"

"That's right, Artie. You're stuck with your family your whole life. You gotta keep the peace no matter what."

Arthur nodded. "A noble sacrifice."

"I'm not gonna have my brother mad at me for the next thirty years. Should we live that long, God willing."

"That's fine, Sal," his wife added. "And the best thing is, after a few years, that round table'll be the tradition, and everybody'll be just as proud."

Sal clasped his palms together. "Amen."

After dinner, Mickey and Arthur took Rocky for a walk, and spent the rest of the evening playing video games. Arthur was especially taken by Joust, at which he was determined to become an expert. Mickey thought it was peculiar that Arthur seemed unfamiliar with the game, but he didn't mention it.

Casey and Arthur spent the next few days going through Arthur's story as they searched for some meaningful detail to pin their hopes on. They picked it apart over and over, but no fact or instance seemed as significant as the name Flatbush. If there were another obvious piece to the puzzle, they just weren't seeing it. By the end of the school week, they were as baffled as ever and completely out of new ideas. It looked as if Arthur might never get back to his own time and place. Arthur was getting used to being a normal, modern day high school teenager, and if he were anyone else the prospect of staying there for the rest of his life might not seem so terrible. But his place in history was essential and unalterable, and he had to end his quest and return home as soon as possible.

To obscure his confusion and pessimism, Casey made sure that Arthur was too busy to worry about his fate. Casey, Mickey, Kevin and Sean introduced him to pizza, bowling, NFL football, movies, TV shows and cartoons, and the wonderful junk food havens of White Castle Hamburgers, Carvel Ice Cream and Taco Bell.

They also taught Arthur how to ride a bike, which he found similar to riding a horse. He took to this quite naturally as a result, and even came up with a game similar to Joust. They were playing a kind of street polo, using old brooms to knock a softball into opposing goals. When Arthur and Casey struggled for the ball and started dueling each other with their broom handles, Arthur suggested that they forget about the ball and try to knock each other off their bicycles.

The game developed quickly, until it was determined that the two opponents would start about fifty feet apart, then ride towards each other as fast as they could. At the last moment, each would lower their brooms and level them over the bike's handlebars, and try to knock the other off the bike without losing his balance and falling himself. The more they played this game, the more they wanted to play it and become as good as they could. Arthur took the contest as seriously as he had the fight with Frank Mayo, though he was aware that it was a game and his opponents were his friends. He truly wanted to win, but he understood more acutely with every round that the skill and control involved were more important. There was honor and nobility in these disciplines, and Arthur wanted to develop them far beyond any paltry notions of winning and losing.

On Friday after school, they all hurried home to drop off their books and met back at Mickey's house. That evening marked the beginning of the Atlantic Avenue festival, a huge street fair which brought people from miles around all weekend. There were rides, shooting galleries, games of chance, street performers, arts and crafts, live music, cheap clothing, second-hand junk, and best of all, booth after booth of great food, prepared on the spot. Just about everyone from school was going, and Casey thought it would be something different and exciting for Arthur. Arthur was used to the idea of not going home for a while, but Casey was running out of diversions. He was afraid of how Arthur might finally react when they had no more leads and ideas of how to get him back where he belonged. He was also aware that they couldn't conceal and protect him indefinitely, and their luck might eventually come to an end.

The fair was in Mickey's neighborhood, not far from his house. They all told their parents that they'd be there until late, and not to expect them for dinner. Casey's mother warned him against eating everything in sight, although she knew that was half the reason everyone went to a street fair. Indeed, as smart and sensible as he was, Casey always made it his goal to try as many things as possible, even if it made him too sick to sleep. Between all the food, the rides and the excitement, it was a challenge for anyone not to indulge himself to the point of nauseous delirium.

On the way, Casey explained to Arthur that the fair had been started by the local parish of the Catholic Church, which still used it to raise money. Arthur took this very seriously, but Mickey added that nobody really cared about that stuff, for they just wanted an excuse to eat, play games and have fun. "It's the only way they can get people to give it money."

Arthur nodded. "It seems that such things never change. When the traveling fairs would pass through my village, I and my fellows would pick a few pockets. The friar would scold us and try to get us to give him the money, but we knew where those coins would likely end up."

When they reached Court and Atlantic as evening fell, the crowd was already dense and increasing rapidly. But it was not the vast numbers of people that struck Arthur, but the overwhelming conflagration of noise, light and activity. The sidewalks were lined with stalls hawking food and games, each one with its own variety of sound effects, and people filled the center of the wide street as barkers called to them non-stop. The bright colored lights of the rides flickered and bounced off the brick apartment buildings, and Italian folk and pop music seemed to come from every direction.

Arthur stopped to take it all in. "Ah, 'tis a wonder to behold!"

"They got these all over the city," Kevin boasted.

"Even in Manhattan," Sean added.

The boys were drawn to the nearest food stall. Paying no attention to order or common sense, they started off with cotton candy all around. Arthur ate his with his fingers in a constant state of disbelief. He couldn't accept that this light pink confection was nothing but strands of spun sugar. He looked closely at each piece before he stuffed it into his mouth, then stared at his sticky fingertips to examine the residue.

"'Tis the greatest invention I've seen yet," he announced confidently.

"It's just cotton candy," Casey said.

"To think that if I go home, such a marvel won't exist for a thousand more years." Casey was calmly stunned by his use of the word if. No one else reacted to the slip, including Arthur.

"What candy do ya have?" Mickey asked.

Arthur considered the question for a few moments. "But for honey cakes at Christmas, only dry fruit."

Sean made a sour face and stuck out his tongue.

Mickey shook his head. "Sounds healthy."

They followed this with a feast of sausage and peppers, root beer and a half dozen Italian donuts with powdered sugar called zeppoles, which they split between them. As they squeezed through the crowd licking white sugar from their greasy fingertips, a keen search began for something else to do.

"Let's play some games," Mickey decided. "That's what I'm here for."

"Yeah," Kevin agreed.

There was no shortage of games, each designed to rope in eager young players to test their skill. When they reached the midway, where the game booths were lined up, Mickey went straight to the basketball hoop. He shelled out a dollar for three shots.

"This looks pretty easy," he said confidently.

"Sure kid," the barker said with a smirk. "My gran'mother could make 'em from there." The hoop was only about ten feet away, and only about six feet off the ground. Mickey set himself and made each shot with expert precision. The balls lofted in a perfect arch towards the center of the basket, where they all hit the rim and bounced out. Mickey was stunned.

"Damn! They shoulda gone right in."

"Guess not. Tough luck, kid."

"Lemme try," Kevin said and muscled his way up to the counter to pay his money and take his shots. Basketball was his best sport after football, but he didn't come close. "I bet they don't even fit!" he complained.

"Sure they do," the barker said. "Whadaya think?" He casually grabbed one of the balls and flipped it underhanded into the air, where it dropped through the basket with ease. "Try again?" he offered.

The boys walked away without a word. "There's gotta be a trick to it," Casey said finally. He was right, of course. The basket was slightly smaller than a regulation hoop. It was also tilted up just enough to make the angle nearly impossible to negotiate from the counter. The barker had made the shot because he was a few feet closer, and had tossed it in from the side, a subtle but crucial difference. In the course of the day, only two people would actually make a basket, out of over a thousand shots.

Their journey to nearly every other game brought the same result. Casey failed to shoot a red star out of the center of a white target with a rifle that shot a stream of metal bits. Sean and Kevin couldn't puncture one balloon with a dart in twelve chances between them. None of the boys could knock over a stack of milk bottles with a seemingly endless supply of baseballs. It went on and on, for each game had its hidden gimmick to virtually ensure loss by the unsuspecting. Few prizes were won, and no one in the crowd ever walked away with any of the bigger items.

Arthur watched this all with detachment. He was amused by the goading assurance of the barkers and the hidden trickiness of their simple challenges. It even made him nostalgic, conjuring up memories of the traveling shows that came to his part of the countryside. He'd seen many overconfident villagers walk away in astonishment at similar contests. He and his friends had even shilled for a few of them, being allowed to win a few times to make the games appear honest. Arthur had become a firm believer in the recently coined adage, A fool and his money are soon parted.

But after a while, such dishonesty began to

seem blatant and petty, no longer merely good sport. The modern setting rendered the impersonal relationship between barker and player stark and extreme. Arthur could sense the anger and disappointment, not only in his friends' experiences, but in those of random strangers as they stormed off in loss and failure. These simple contests for cheap trinkets ceased to be about winning and losing. They began to overwhelm Arthur with their lack of fairness. It was cruel and unnecessary. Arthur realized that most people would lose anyway, and found all this deception and selfishness abominable. It must not be, he concluded. The world should be nothing if not fair and honest.

21

he boys moved on, their spirits dampened severely. It took no less than another assault on the food stalls to restore their enthusiasm. After some fried clams in tartar sauce and fried calamari in hot sauce, they cooled off with sno-cones. Then it was time for a few rides. They warmed up on the mini-roller-coaster, which they all agreed was nothing compared to the Cyclone at Coney Island. As they waited on line for the big Tilt-a-Whirl, Sean wondered if they should wait a while, since they'd all just eaten.

"What for?" Kevin asked.

"So we don't barf."

"Don't worry."

"Yeah," Mickey added. "By the time we get to the front of the line, we'll be okay." As they advanced, the ride seemed to get faster and more volatile. By the time they were about to get aboard, it appeared too big and scary to survive at all.

Sean looked at its metal panels and exposed machinery and started to back away.

"Where ya going?" Kevin demanded.

"I don't know, Kev. I still feel full."

"After the rollercoaster?"

"That's different."

"You're just scared."

"I am not! I been on the Tilt-a-Whirl before!"

"We have to drag you every time."

"Hey, if he's gonna throw up, maybe we should wait," Mickey offered.

"Then he's gonna go alone, 'cause I'm not waitin' all over again."

"Awright, forget it."

The attendant opened the gate and swiftly ushered them on.

Nobody wanted to stand next to Sean, for fear that he might get nauseous. But they were all directed into place and strapped down without consideration. As the huge steel cylinder began to move, Casey, Kevin and Mickey kept their eyes on Sean, hoping he'd be able to hang on till the end.

Before the Tilt-a-Whirl even reached top speed, they were all scared. Indeed, with eyes closed and teeth clenched, much too scared and frozen stiff to be nauseous. But this was part of the fun. When the machine was spinning so ferociously that its participants could no longer think straight and the maddening, rapid fire sound of the wind in their ears magically slipped away, the machine performed its ultimate feat. Its floor dropped out for ten endless seconds.

Arthur began to black out. He felt just as he did when he'd been transported in time. Then he had a premonition, a vision. The world and all time and space fell away and something came towards him out of the black void. It achieved an instant of crisp focus, and then it seemed to pass through him with a sharp chill and a grating, twisted laugh. It was the witch, Melora, and somewhere in the furthest reaches of that hideous cackle was a whispered sound; two words, uttered and lost in the maelstrom of nothingness. A message that Arthur could not decipher.

"Arthur, y'okay?"

"Uh-oh."

"Hey, come on."

Arthur opened his eyes and stumbled forward. Casey helped him off the still Tilt-a-Whirl. "The ride's over. You okay?"

"I think he's gonna barf," Sean said.

"Shut up."

Arthur rubbed his eyes and looked around, as if reacquainting himself with his surroundings.

"Guess that thing was too much for you," Casey offered with a hopeful grin.

"Something happened. I had a... a vision."

"Of what?"

"I saw Melora. She said something to me. Like a message."

Sean and Kevin exchanged bewildered looks.

"Wow," Mickey cried. "What'd it say?"

Arthur shook his head. "I could not understand it. It seemed like two words, '*oo ee*,' but... "

His voice trailed off and he didn't try to finish, but repeated the sounds to himself over and over. Oo-ee, oo-ee, oo-ee...

"Maybe that's the sign we've been waiting for," Casey announced ominously. They walked away from the ride and rejoined the crowd. Casey got Arthur a drink of cold water, to help him clear his head. He seemed woozy, but Casey knew him well enough now to detect that Arthur was also distracted. His vision or message, or whatever it was, had deeply affected him. He no longer appeared ready to go back to having fun. "Maybe we should just go home, Arthur."

"No, I'm all right. T'would make no difference."

Casey shrugged. He felt useless. He wished that he'd had the vision instead. They wandered along, idly watching a pair of jugglers and then a magician perform for a while. Then they moved on and discovered the tables of second-hand clothes, antiques and collectibles. There were toys and games that Casey and his friends found old-fashioned, even though they were only ten years old. It was hard for them to imagine themselves playing with such junk. But there were also more recent toys, some of which they had played with and could still be found in their attics and basements. It was a peculiar sight, as if little pieces of their childhoods had been put on display.

None of this meant anything to Arthur. He might have been curious to examine these colorful plastic oddities. But he was still preoccupied by his experience on the Tilt-a-Whirl. He'd been set adrift in a dense, hazy limbo. He felt like the weight of his destiny was being further pressed upon him. It was not merely that his journey and his future were in jeopardy, but his very identity. It was as if Arthur the king and Arthur the legend had come to confront Arthur the lost boy, defying him to unify his far-flung components and become his true self, once and for all. Arthur was being challenged, but he was still unaware of the nature of the contest.

Arthur wandered away from Casey and the gang. He was drawn to the edge of the crowd, where an a old woman sat at a small round table. She wore a drab flowing purple dress, with faded red scarves on her head and around her neck. There were old bracelets on her arms and cheap rings on her bony fingers. When the river of people thinned out for a few seconds, Arthur caught a glimpse of her withered face.

He froze. It was Melora!

She looked right at him and their eyes met. He thought she grinned slightly and he broke free of the crowd and raced forward. When Arthur stopped and stood right over her, she turned to him and looked up hopefully.

"Yes?"

But it was not the Duke's old witch. Close up, she was just an old woman dressed as a fortune teller. "You want a reading?" she asked dryly. "Only three dollars." She began to reach out. But before her tentative fingertips could make contact with Arthur's hand, he took off again. He was disappointed and disoriented and didn't know where to go. Arthur stood in the center of the crowd as people passed him on all sides going in every direction.

Arthur had already been lost. But now he was no longer connected to the slips of territory with which he'd become familiar. He felt hopelessly cut off from his home and time, and yet dauntingly surrounded by them as well. It was as if the past, present and future had all rose up and fused around him. The atmosphere of the festival, with its conflagration of sounds and activities and attractions, was just like similar events at home. Arthur closed his eyes and imagined being back there, knowing full well that he was not. He could feel them. He could feel his time and place and the need to summon them to him at that very moment. He could feel that Arthur rejoin the one he was now...

22

rthur?" a soft voice called. "It's me."
He did not respond.
"Arthur, it's Theresa." He turned at the sound of his name.

She approached tentatively, for his face failed to register any sign of recognition. "Are you all right?" She came up to him and touched him lightly on the arm.

His eyes found the precious gold cross at her throat. For a few seconds, it was all he could see. Then he looked up and was taken by the deep concern in her dark eyes. "Oh, Theresa. Hello."

"You don't look well."

"Oh, yes. I fear I've feasted beyond all reason."

She nodded, smiling. "That's the problem with these things."

She glanced around to indicate the entire festival. "You just can't help yourself and always regret it later. Just ask this one." She looked down with a critical smirk.

It was then that Arthur noticed a little boy standing next to her, holding her hand. Their eyes met and they stared at each other in silent disinterest, as if they were too far apart to communicate.

"This is my little brother, Peter. He wants to eat everything sight, too."

"Not everything," he protested.

"I gave up trying not to spoil his dinner. But he'll be sorry later when he gets sick and has nightmares."

"I will not." He frowned and stared at the ground, as if trying to bear up under this torrent of insults. "Anyway I wanna throw the rings and win the big dog. Let's go." He pulled desperately on her arm.

"He wants to play the ring toss," she explained. "The best prize is a big red stuffed dog." Theresa turned away from Peter and whispered so he couldn't hear her. "I keep trying to stall him so he'll forget about it."

"Oh?" Arthur echoed her solemn tone, although he had no idea what she was talking about.

"It looks too hard and I'm afraid he'll be disappointed. Then he'll cry about it all weekend."

Arthur nodded. He understood now. But it was hard for him to maintain his grim concern. It was so insignificant, whether this child won or lost and went home with any prize at all. Arthur had other things to worry about, such as the repeated appearance of Melora. He wasn't even sure if he'd really seen her or if he was so desperate for a sign that he'd been hallucinating. Had it really been her, she could just be taunting him or trying to lead him astray. He didn't know what to think now, he was so lost and bewildered.

"Let's go-o, Terry," Peter pleaded and pulled his sister's hand. He would not give up.

"Okay, okay." Theresa looked at Arthur helplessly. "I guess he's gotta play it, no matter what." She sighed as the boy started making progress. She moved a few steps in the direction of the game booths. "Well, maybe it'll be a good lesson for him that he just can't have everything he wants."

"Come on." Peter looked back at Theresa to get her moving again, and Arthur caught sight of his face. He looked like Arthur felt, desperate and hopeful, as if his whole life were about to be measured by this one contest.

Well, maybe... Arthur had begun to think that with a little luck, the boy just might win. Then he realized that the game was no more honest than the rest of them and he was doomed to lose, like everyone else. There was a sharp pang in his gut. "Theresa, I must warn you... "

"Yes?"

He wanted to tell her of the game's trickery and that Peter had no chance at all. But the boy was now dragging her towards the booths. "Let me go with you." Arthur followed, hoping he could think of a way to alter this impending disaster. It mattered not that the boy might win or lose. The outcome was irrelevant, for the contest was not fair.

For some reason, Arthur just could not let this injustice pass.

"Hey, Arthur, where you been?" Mickey asked. They ran into Casey and his friends half way to their destination. "Oh, hi Theresa." Mickey glanced from her to Arthur with a slight smirk.

"I can't hold him back," she said to Arthur. She turned as Peter continued to haul her off.

"So ya ditched us for her, huh," Mickey joked. "I knew she liked you."

"I'm just worried about her young brother. He's determined to win that grand prize and the game is a bloody sham. I must do something." He walked after them without waiting for a response.

"We should stay close behind them," Casey said. He didn't like the look on Arthur's face. But he'd seen it before, at the fight with Frank Mayo. Arthur seemed to be going into battle once again.

"Think Theresa has any idea about Arthur?" Mickey asked. "I mean, you know." Mickey made a weird face and pointed to the side of his head.

Casey knew what he meant, but didn't say a thing. He'd told her about Arthur's situation that first day of school. But that seemed a long time ago and Casey no longer believed that simple explanation himself.

While Peter and Theresa waited their turn among a small crowd of spectators, Arthur watched a few players step up to the counter at the ring toss and try their luck. He stared at the repeated actions of the game like a field general looking down into a valley of enemy troops. He was searching for some way to beat the game on its own terms. But there was nothing to find, for Arthur already knew this game well. Neither he nor Casey and the others had played it before, but Arthur knew the game from a similar version back home. Indeed, it was virtually indistinguishable from its medieval predecessor. It was a simple peg-and-ring set up, with a vertical board of fifty numbered pegs and three rings. The only things that had changed in a thousand years were the prizes and the make-up of the rings, which were heavy plastic instead of wood.

Although some players managed to hang a few rings, no ring ended up on the pegs with the numbers corresponding to the better prizes. This was no surprise to Arthur, for the gimmick also hadn't changed in ten centuries. The pegs with the big winning numbers were just close enough to the losing pegs that it was impossible to toss a ring onto them without hitting a neighboring peg, making it bounce off. There was only enough space between the pegs with the worst numbers.

Peter stepped up to the counter and Theresa paid three dollars for nine rings. "Now don't rush it," she warned. "Take your time. This is all the money we have left."

"I know, I know."

"That's right kid," the barker instructed. "This is the easiest game out here." He was tall and thin, and he grinned and winked at Arthur with impunity, as if letting him in on the deception.

"Wait," Theresa announced. "He wants to win

the big dog. Just to make sure, which number is that?"

"Seventeen. The kid's gotta get all three on there to win it. Got that, chief?"

Peter nodded, his mouth half open in intense childish concentration as he got ready to play. He searched for the peg with the number seventeen painted on the end. The numbers were in random order, and he finally spotted it up near the left hand corner of the board. Theresa supportively placed her hands lightly on Peter's shoulders, then removed them when he quickly shook them off.

"Stand back, folks," the barker said with a smirk. "This kid's not going home empty-handed."

The bastard, Arthur thought murderously. He knew he couldn't lose and relished the boy's pathetic determination. It was monstrous. If he'd had his sword, Arthur would've found enormous satisfaction in running him through on the spot for his arrogance.

Peter leaned forward and rose up on his tip-toes. When he was ready to throw, he bit his lip and let the first ring fly. It hit the middle of the peg board hard and bounced off. Theresa clucked her tongue and her whole body shook at the miss. She seemed more pessimistic and disappointed than her brother, who remained focused and confident. He had eight shots left and was just warming up. He threw the second ring, which actually hit the bottom of the number seventeen peg before it rico-cheted downward. Peter flinched and Theresa cried, "Oh!"

Arthur was silent, but it was surprising that he'd got so close so quickly. It almost allowed him to think that Peter had a real chance. But this was as close as the kid would get. He missed with his third, fourth and fifth rings completely. Then he stopped and wiped his sweaty, nervous hands on his pants and got set again. The next ring arced towards the board and hung perfectly on the number five peg. By now Casey and the others had joined the small crowd of on-lookers. There were a few cheers and a round of applause.

Theresa was ecstatic. "You got one!" She clasped her hands together as if it were suddenly no contest. But her enthusiasm flagged immediately when she realized that Peter had only three shots left and would have to make all of them to win the dog.

Arthur's hands were clenched at his sides and his jaw was locked tight. The crowd pushed in a little closer as Peter worked up his concentration, his eyes fixed on that winning peg.

The barker stood to the side, watching him with subdued anticipation, as if he might actually be pulling for the kid. Theresa kept her fingers crossed and whispered, "Come on, come on," over and over. At the last moment, she took her small gold cross in her fingertips and silently brought it to her lips. Despite the irreverent occasion, certainly a prayer could do no harm.

Peter waited and held his breath as if he might never be ready. Then he tossed the seventh ring with a flick of his wrist. But he'd held onto it for too long and it fell far short of the board and bounced on the platform in front of it.

"Oh no!" Theresa cried.

For a moment, Peter had no reaction. Then his face sagged and he threw the last two rings as if he didn't care at all. The last one hung on the edge of the peg numbered thirty-five and wobbled to a stop.

"Number thirty-five!" the barker cried. He reached up to the first shelf of prizes and found the one that matched the number. He set a cheap cigarette lighter on the counter in front of Peter. "A winner!"

Peter looked down at this pitiful consolation prize. After a moment, he picked it up and held it a few inches from his face. Theresa set her hands on her little brother's shoulders. She looked more disappointed than he did.

The barker clapped his hands and searched the crowd. "Who's next?"

Arthur stepped forward. He intended to play the game himself, but when he reached the counter he was too angry and couldn't contain himself. "'Tis not a fair gambit. He could not win." He scowled up at the man.

"What was that?"

"'Tis not possible to win. This game is unfair, sir." Arthur stared at him defiantly, refusing to move or blink.

The facade of cheer left the man's face, making him seem lean and feral. "Hey, kid, you can't win 'em all. That's just the way it is. Don't be a sore loser, huh."

"The rings don't fit on the winning pegs!" Arthur

shouted, attracting more attention.

"Sure they do. Whadaya think!"

"Not for the best prizes!" Arthur's anger had exceeded the juvenile petulance that he'd exhibited at the Duke's castle. His objection to the situation had wisdom and maturity, a moral force that came from arguing on another's behalf. This was no personal attack or quest for revenge. It was a matter of justice, a principle that must apply to all.

"It's okay, Arthur," Theresa said, surprised at his sudden vigilance. "It's just a stupid game."

"But it is not. If there's no way to win than it's no more than simple thievery."

"Ay, you calling me a thief, kid?" The barker hovered over Arthur with his hands on his hips, trying to intimidate him. He'd put the boy on the spot and was staring him down.

"I need not call you a thief, for you are a thief!"

Casey had gotten increasingly nervous at this display. He kept waiting for Arthur to back off. He couldn't believe he was making such a big deal out of this. Casey looked around, hoping that none of the cops patrolling the fair had noticed the commotion. If one showed up, Arthur was doomed.

"You got a beef, then call a cop. I run an honest game and nobody's complained but you." He held up his arms as if he were being more than reasonable. But he was just calling Arthur's bluff.

Arthur was on a mission now and would not be dissuaded. His change was nearly complete. This conflict was not about him. Fairness and honesty were to be enforced, not for the glory of those who could stand up and fight for themselves, like he had against Frank Mayo. No, they were for the small and weak, the helpless and anonymous, like Peter, who was no threat at all. There was a supreme truth in this, Arthur realized, a code of living. He was possessed with determination as never before, as if his righteousness would protect him from that moment on.

"Cop!" Arthur demanded, confident even in the modern vernacular. "Cop, here!"

"Arthur, no!" Casey cried as if his worst fears were about to swallow them all. As others echoed the call for the nearest policeman, Casey grabbed Arthur's arm and pulled him back a few steps.

"You've gotta run!"

"I can do no such thing, my friend."

"What if he asks you who you are and where you live?"

"Than I shall tell him. I shan't hide from my true self any longer. What king will not honestly proclaim his name from every mountaintop?"

Casey buried his face in his hands. It was too late. He could see Arthur being dragged off no matter what he did. Casey expected the worst. He would never see Arthur again.

The barker looked a little nervous. He'd been in this situation before. He'd been sure that Arthur wouldn't go this far and now he couldn't back down himself.

"Awright, what's the problem here?" A large, barrel-chested police officer divided the crowd with the power of Moses. He pushed his way up to the counter and leaned on it with nearly all his weight. He was almost twice as wide as the thin barker and bent over into his face, impatient for an explanation. "Well?"

Arthur squeezed back into the fray and immediately made his presence known without humility. "'Tis this game, sir. This boy here spent his last dollar in the hope of winning that big red dog." Arthur laid a firm hand on Peter's small shoulder. "But the contest is dishonest and cannot be won."

The officer made a stern face, not taking his eyes off the shifty barker. "What about it, pal?"

He grinned defensively. "Come on, you know how it is. I'm tryin' to make a living here."

"Yeah, I know how it is. But you're supposed to give 'em half a chance." The barker ran through his repertoire of grins, smirks and smiles, searching for the best one under the circumstances. "You ever give away any of that stuff?" The cop nodded up at the shelf with the big red dog and the other top prizes.

"You gotta get all three rings for them, not just one. This ain't no charity."

"The rings will fit on none of those pegs," Arthur spat in controlled outrage.

The cop looked down. "Just who're you?"

Casey went cold. He saw the cop's expression as his gaze focused entirely on Arthur. This was it. He knew what Arthur was about to say and what would happen when he did. They'd never get him out of this one. He couldn't even rely on Theresa to pick up on the situation and save him.

"Arthur, King of England," he said with unmistakable clarity and volume.

The cop nodded. "Arthur King, of England," he repeated with a slightly different emphasis. "What're you, visiting or something?"

It was a miracle. Casey recognized the chance and took it. "He's my cousin!" he blurted out, coming forward. "He's with me, Casey Hanson. And this is Peter—" The cop looked at Casey and waved him off. As Casey had hoped, the torrent of names was too much for him and beside the point.

The cop made a decision and looked back at the barker. "Okay, lemme see you put a ring on that peg, the one that gets the dog." He folded his arms and waited.

The man hesitated, then picked up a ring and tried to toss it onto the number seventeen peg as if it were an easy fit. He had a little trouble and tried again, with another ring a few steps closer. It hit the peg below it and fell off. He caught it and was forced to step a little closer this time. Glancing back at the waiting cop, who wouldn't give an inch, the barker carefully laid it on the very edge of the peg. But it still wouldn't fit. When he finally stepped right up to the board and pressed it between the surrounding pegs, bending it into the tight space, it stayed. It wasn't actually touching the number seventeen peg, but was held securely around it.

The barker stepped aside with embarrassment. He shook his head and cursed and the crowd cheered and applauded. The cop nodded and laughed.

Then he glanced at Arthur and said, "You're right, kid. It's impossible unless you jam it in there from a foot away."

Arthur was tempted to reiterate his point. It would emphasize his triumph and compound the man's comeuppance. But he just remained quiet and let the outcome speak for itself.

The barker shrugged helplessly. "Whadaya want from me, huh?"

The cop glanced up at the top shelf. "Just that big dog."

"What?"

"Give the little guy that dog and take out a few of those pegs."

"Hey, come on—"

"You want a summons along with it? Give him the dog or it'll cost you a hundred bucks on top of it."

The barker sighed and took the big red stuffed dog off the shelf and set it on the counter in front of Peter. He sneered at Arthur as he stepped back, but it was such a futile gesture that it made him look worse. "Satisfied?"

The cop pointed a finger at him. "I'll be back later to check on those pegs. I may even play the thing myself." Then he turned and wandered off, joining the crowd as it quickly dispersed.

Peter took the dog off the counter, his face alight with joy. It was almost as big as he was. He'd already forgot the whole sour experience of having excitedly played the game and lost so miserably.

"Oh, Arthur, I can't believe it." Theresa clutched her hands to her chest. She looked at him, almost mesmerized by his quiet confidence and pure humility.

"T'was merely what was right. No more."

"But still. Thank you. I can't... I mean... " Theresa didn't know what to do, so she just leaned over and kissed Arthur on the cheek. "We have to go. I guess I'll see you later."

Arthur watched her back away. He bowed his head slightly. "Fair lady."

"Let's go, Peter." She took his wrist and led him off. The boy's short arms were wrapped around the big dog and he struggled to hold on to it. "Say goodbye to Arthur," she instructed him at the last minute.

"Bye!" he called awkwardly behind him.

23

The ordeal took the life out of the fair for Casey. He was sweating and his heart was pounding and he didn't have the energy to stay another minute, so he started to leave. Mickey and Arthur joined him, and Kevin and Sean had little choice but to follow. Suddenly, the fun had gone out of the entire occasion and there was nothing to do but go home.

"Don't forget about tomorrow," Casey said to Arthur as they all parted company not far from Mickey's house. He knew that Arthur now felt invulnerable and expected to be rewarded for his actions at the fair. But Casey realized that he might not receive an immediate sign of return. No matter how confident and transformed Arthur might be, Casey was more worried about his fate than ever. Either he was on the verge of magnificent triumph, or catastrophic failure.

Fortunately, Casey already had Saturday covered. It was the day that Arthur was to go with

Casey and his father to pick up their new car. It seemed a trivial undertaking, considering Arthur's state of mind. But Casey wasn't prepared to let him go off on his own in search of divine guidance. Indeed, he was afraid to let him out of his sight.

The car dealership was on the other side of Flatbush Avenue, in the business district. On the way, Casey explained to Arthur that the dealer would take his dad's old one and give him a new one. It seemed suspicious to Arthur, until Casey's father remarked that his old car was worth only a tenth of the new one, so he'd have to pay the difference. Now Arthur understood completely, and wondered if the arrangement couldn't somehow be applied to horses as well.

"What would you do with the old horses?" Casey asked.

"What do they do with the old cars?"

"They sell them to people who can't afford new ones," Casey's father said firmly.

"Ah, I see," Arthur concluded. "Then we could sell the old horses to the poor, who have none."

Casey's father laughed. "I don't know, Arthur. Trading in the old car is really just a little incentive to get you to give up the cash for a new one. It's a favor to sweeten the deal."

Arthur thought about this seriously on the rest of the way. It sounded okay on the surface. But he couldn't help but detect an unsavory aspect underneath. There was something dishonest and evasive about the arrangement. It sounded unjust, he decided. Why couldn't the purchase be direct and beyond discussion? Arthur wondered. The words that Casey's father had used were particularly awful and revealing. *Sweeten* the deal. Arthur couldn't imagine such a notion occupying the heads of men who could look each other in the eye as they shook hands.

The car dealership was the most beautiful place that Arthur had ever seen. As familiar as the modern world was to him now, he'd never even imagined such a paradise. These shiny metal carriages were a true marvel. The colors were so bright and pure, and Arthur could actually see his reflection in them. He could understand the temptation of buying a new car, to which Casey's father had succumbed. Casey and his father walked among the models in the showroom as if temporarily mesmerized by each of them. But when they finally stopped at a particular one near the center of the big open room, Casey's father ran his hand gingerly over its immaculate black finish.

"Is this it?" Casey asked. "It's huge, Dad."

"Yup, the new Excalibur. Beautiful, isn't she?"

"Excalibur," Arthur echoed. "What a wonderful sound. *Ex...cal...ibur,*" he said again slowly. I should have something called this, he thought. Such a word could make one invincible.

A dapper looking salesman appeared and shook Casey's father's hand. He announced that the car was here and was just out back. Then he handed him the new set of keys, which hung from a ring shaped like a small sword. Casey's father thanked the salesman and he ushered them to the rear, where the exit let out onto a huge lot filled with new and old cars. The new black Excalibur was parked at the end of a row of shiny new models waiting to be picked up. The salesman asked Casey's father if he needed anything else and took the keys to his old car. They shook hands again and the salesman wished him luck and told him to drive safely.

"Let's go, boys."

Casey and Arthur ran to the car and got in. "Wow, smell that new-car smell," Casey cried. They closed the doors as Casey's father got in slowly, savoring the moment. "Come on, Dad, start her up."

"Relax, ya only get to pick up a new car once. It's a ritual that shouldn't be rushed." He started the car, which roared to life with supreme power. He let it idle for a few moments, then smoothly backed out of the space and drove out of the lot. "Why don't we drive a little. Take the scenic route."

"Yeah," Casey agreed. "No rush, right?"

His father couldn't hide his grin. Then he stepped on the gas and car picked up speed. Before they knew it, the streets were flying by.

The inside of the car seemed cavernous. Its plush black upholstery enveloped Casey and Arthur, and protected them from the outside world. Casey could barely hear the engine or feel the street beneath the tires. He couldn't even hear the street sounds beyond the windows. He felt like he was in a compact black rocket ship, hurdling towards worlds unknown. Casey marveled at the interior of the new Excalibur. It was immaculate, as if the car had been made yesterday, specially for them. All the controls were right at their fingertips, and as Casey played with the ashtray, perfectly hidden in the sleek armrest beside him, he couldn't think of a thing that the car lacked. He was ready to live in it.

"Whadaya think, Arthur? Pretty cool, huh?"

Arthur nodded. "'Tis royal indeed."

Casey grinned. "Fit for a king!"

Arthur laughed. "Even King Arthur."

Casey's father opened the automatic window and the cool air flowed in. "So boys, where do ya wanna go?"

"Just drive, Dad. It doesn't matter if we ever get home."

"Why don't we head up Flatbush. It's a nice long street and we can really cruise."

Casey's father swung the car around and they were off. Flatbush Avenue ran about ten miles through the center of Brooklyn. It ran through at least ten different neighborhoods, from the tip of the borough on the East River, through quiet and residential Park Slope, through regal Grand Army Plaza and the crowded business district, past creaky old East Flatbush, all the way to the naval base on the shores of the Rockaway Inlet. Casey had his head on his folded arms, which were resting on the edge of the door. His eyes were fixed on the view from his window. From all the different people and streets and buildings that passed by, Casey got a renewed sense of the size and complexity of the place he lived in. It was immense and full of variety, with a proud history. Casey rarely had cause to leave the small area of his own neighborhood and those around it. It was easy for him to forget just how vast and unconquerable Brooklyn really was, and that it had once been a thriving city all its own, independent of the four other boroughs that now officially formed New York City. By the time they reached the southern reaches of Flatbush Avenue, near the Flatlands, Casey had probably seen more of Brooklyn in the last hour than he'd seen in his whole life.

Arthur, too, was affected. From his place of privilege in the shiny new car he saw people he recognized as poor, wearing ragged clothes and begging in front of rundown buildings, or warming their hands over fires burning in rusty steel barrels. He vowed then that as long as he was on the throne, his people would never be forced to endure such a state of hopeless indignity.

"Why don't we swing around and head home," his father announced, breaking the spell.

Casey had heard him but said nothing. He didn't want the ride to end.

"Come on kiddo, we can't stay in the car forever. If I don't turn around now we'll be in Queens."

Casey groaned. "Okay."

"Don't worry, we can still take our time. That okay with you, Arthur?"

"Oh, yes. That's fine, sir."

Casey's father slowed down and pulled over. He waited for the traffic to thin out, then he made a U-turn and started going north on Flatbush again. As the car began to pick up speed, they approached a small side street that resembled an old country road. At the far corner was a sign, Dead End. At the near one the street sign was bent and hidden by the branch of a huge tree. When they were just about at the mouth of the side street, Casey caught a glimpse of the faded name on the sign.

Duke Street.

Casey almost jumped out of the car window. "Dad wait! Turn here!"

"What?!" He looked around frantically for an emergency.

"Stop, quick! This street! You gotta go in there! Arthur, look at the sign. Duke Street."

Arthur looked up and his eyes went wide with recognition. Oo-ee, D-oo-ke Str-ee-t. "That's it," he said, turning to Casey. "The words Melora whispered in the vision. I'm sure of it."

Casey grinned. They finally had a lead.

Casey's father pulled over quickly. "Why do you suddenly wanna go down there?" He peered into the entrance to the dim corridor. "It's a dead end. Can't you see the sign?"

"Just... trust me, Dad. Take this street. I just hafta check something out. I'll take two seconds."

"I've never even heard of Duke Street."

"Dad," he insisted.

"Okay, relax. But you have to tell me what you're looking for."

Casey was afraid that he'd ask this question.

"It's kinda hard to explain." He glanced back at Arthur, hoping that he'd think of something to say.

"Come on Case, what's the big secret?"

"I wish I knew," Arthur whispered.

"It's something me and Arthur're doing for school," Casey blurted out. "We're supposed to do the history of a street." The history of a street! he thought. You couldn't come up with something better than that?

His father nodded. "Sounds interesting. Why Duke Street?"

He hit the turn signal and prepared to make the sharp right turn.

"The teacher picked it out. I never heard of it either, but she said it was one of the oldest streets in Brooklyn. So I figured there'd be lots to write about."

"Well, let's hope so. It doesn't look like much from here." The car entered the small inlet, which indeed seemed neglected and cut off from the rest of the area. "Looks pretty run down to me. Like history's passed it by."

The pavement was broken up and the few buildings along the street were dilapidated and abandoned. They appeared to have been modest stores, like those found in a small town. One of them had the remains of a sign above its door indicating that it had been a grocery store.

"Looks more like the stores you see in old cowboy movies," Casey's father commented. "Imagine, a ghost town right here in Brooklyn."

The stretch of stores ended abruptly and a

string of houses began. There were only a few on the entire street, and all but one was brick. The last house on the block was wood, and it sat at the very end of the street. It was surrounded by a rusty iron fence and faced the dead end, where the shiny new car was forced to come to a stop.

"Well, this is it, boys," Casey's father announced. "I'll bet nobody's lived on this block for years. They should just knock everything down and clear it all out."

Casey and Arthur stared at the small house for a few moments. Then Arthur rolled down his window to get a better look, but he didn't know what he expected to find. There was nothing to see, so Casey opened the door and got out of the car.

"Where you going, Case?"

"I'll only be a second." He stepped out slowly, leaving the car door wide open. Casey carefully walked towards the house. There was an old tin mailbox hanging from the gate, and Casey spotted part of a name in old faded letters. Casey was compelled to keep going. His father called from the car window, wondering what he was doing. Casey didn't respond. Halfway to the house he stopped, a bit scared, but he still couldn't make out the rest of the name and had to walk right up to the gate.

"Casey," his father called, "don't go in there! The place is probably condemned."

But Casey didn't go through the twisted, rusty gate. He only stood there for a second. Just long enough to read the faded letters on the old mailbox. Then he turned and ran back to the car, grinning all the way.

"What were you doing over there?" his father asked, a bit annoyed.

"Looking at the name on the mailbox."

"It actually still says something?"

"Duke," he said giddily, and turned to his friend in the back seat.

"Duke?" His father scowled. "Maybe the guy owned the whole street."

24

asey didn't say a word on the ride back. His face didn't even change. He just stared out the window, thinking about that little shack at the end of Duke Street. The secret to Arthur's entire journey was somewhere in there, and now Casey wished that he'd had the chance to go through the gate and look in the front window. He thought for a moment that the house was some kind of passage in time. But the idea crumbled under the realization that Arthur had appeared in Prospect Park, not on its broken down front step. Still, that house, he thought. What could it be? If only Arthur had recognized something about it.

When Casey's father asked Arthur if he wanted to be dropped off somewhere, Casey snapped out of his trance and said that Arthur had left his stuff at their house, so he had to pick it up before going home. They spent some time up in Casey's room just to make the charade look good, then they came downstairs again. Casey announced that he was going to walk Arthur home, and before anybody could say anything, out they went.

"So whadaya think?" Casey asked as soon as they were free of the house.

"I don't know. But it all tickles the imagination."

"I can't figure it out. Before we left, I looked in the phone book and there were a lotta people named Duke, but none on Duke Street."

"Ah, that must mean something."

"But what, Arthur?! I went over your story in my head a million times, but I couldn't come up with a way that house fits into it."

Arthur nodded. "I too, racked my brain for some tell-tale sign. Maybe it's a trap. I don't trust Melora, even after all these thousand years."

"I guess there's only one way to tell. We'll hafta go into that house." It hadn't occurred to Casey until that very moment, but it was clearly the only solution.

"Agreed. Trap or test, there's no choice. When shall we go?"

"Well, tomorrow's Sunday. There's no school again, so we'll have all day."

They got to Mickey's and Arthur went up the steps and rang the bell. When Mickey opened the door, Arthur turned and waved, his face stoic but pleasant. Casey almost froze. Arthur didn't look like one of his friends or just another teenager. He looked like a king waving farewell. Casey felt his pessimism give way, overwhelmed by Arthur's destiny. He realized that Arthur would probably find a way home eventually. Casey wanted to help him, but he also didn't want to lose his new friend.

They met early the next day. Casey grabbed his bike as soon as he finished breakfast and rode over to Mickey's. Mickey and Arthur were dressed and waiting. Mickey had his bike, and Arthur was using Mickey's brother's, as usual.

"Ready?" Casey asked.

Mickey nodded. "Yeah, let's go."

Casey had almost objected to Mickey's coming. But there had been no good reason to keep the discovery of the house to themselves. Casey had to admit that he wasn't Arthur's only friend, and they were going to need all the help they could get once they got there.

Halfway down the block, Kevin and Sean appeared on their bicycles. Mickey had called them after breakfast. Casey was glad to see them. It was a long ride to the south end of Flatbush Avenue, and a great leap of faith that they would actually find what they were looking for. The size of the group made the search seem more serious, and increased the likelihood of confirmed results. With the five of us, Casey thought, we're sure to find something.

"You remember where this place is?" Kevin asked as the group rode off.

"Of course, we were just there yesterday."

"Just what're we lookin' for?" Sean asked dubiously.

"I don't know, but whatever it is, it's gotta be in there."

Kevin shook his head. "The whole thing sounds pretty... "

"What?"

"Risky," Sean said.

"Weird," Kevin said. They looked at each other in essential agreement. "I thought Arthur wasn't supposed to go home," he whispered to Casey a few moments later.

Casey glanced at Kevin and realized that he and Sean still believed that Arthur was just a lost, confused boy who'd run away from home. They didn't know that Arthur was really... Arthur.

"Don't worry, this is what we gotta do." They peddled up Bergen Street and turned onto Flatbush Avenue. The quest had begun.

The avenue was bustling with activity as the five boys made their way south. Flatbush was the widest and busiest street in Brooklyn, and on Sunday it seemed that the population of the entire borough had converged there at once. Families were out shopping, young couples crowded the brunch spots and old, lifetime residents just walked around to keep active. All the stores were open and there was no shortage of cars going to and fro. The noise was dense and constant.

As they cut through Park Slope, the light changed and the small group was forced to stop at the corner with the rest of the traffic. Casey wished they could keep going, for there was a familiar face at the deli on 7th Avenue, near the stoplight.

It was the first time anyone had seen Frank Mayo since the fight.

He was standing with a few of the losers who always seemed to be hanging out with him, at one place or another. Frank had spotted Arthur and was staring at him, trying to look cool.

"Uh-oh," Mickey said for all of them.

"Yeah," Kevin added. "Think he'll do something?"

Casey squeezed his handle bars tightly. The light would take only thirty seconds to turn green, but the wait seemed endless. Frank was talking out of the side of his mouth to his cronies, and they were looking at Arthur as if trying to size him up.

"Just get ready to move," Casey whispered.

The two groups locked eyes, their faces implacable. Frank looked as if he were about to step forward. Casey looked up at the light. Come on, come on, he thought.

"Better look out Arthur," Mickey warned.

Arthur then turned his head and looked at Frank directly, as if he'd just noticed him standing there. He raised his hand and waved. "Frank, my friend!" he declared in a loud, noble voice. "It's good to see you!" Then he gave him a broad smile.

Frank flinched, then scowled and looked around. He didn't know how to react. He almost returned the greeting, but at the last moment he turned quickly and marched into the deli as if he desperately needed something.

Mickey clapped his hands and laughed. "D'you see that?"

"Wow, Arthur," Kevin said. "He's afraid of you now."

Arthur shook his head. "No, he just doesn't know how to face me as a friend. He wishes that we were still enemies."

Casey was relieved, but he was still a little unnerved. As the light changed and they started off again, the ominous feeling stayed with him. Frank was like a sentry at the edge of their safe little domain. His presence was telling them to be aware as they journeyed on. It was as if they were heading into the dangerous unknown, and they had to be on guard.

They rode in single file, with Casey in front. The long ride was slightly uphill, so they had to peddle all the way. But it kept them all determined, for they couldn't just pick up speed and cruise along freely. They kept their eyes in front of them and didn't speak, as if they wanted to preserve every bit of effort and energy. As Casey led the small party through the heart of Brooklyn, he wondered what the end of the day would bring.

Almost immediately there were obstacles. Cars and pedestrians cut them off. Restaurant delivery boys and bike messengers aggressively competed with them for road space. When they stopped at a traffic light, a homeless man accosted then like a leper for help. A few tough older kids hassled them with inquiries of what they were doing in their neighborhood and where they were going. More than once someone screamed, "Watch where you're going" at them, forcing them to yell back, "Look out," as they passed by. But they kept a good pace, refusing to detour or be delayed for too long.

It took over an hour to reach the far end of Flatbush Avenue. Casey slowed down and began to look for the entrance to Duke Street. "Okay, guys. It's around here somewhere."

"Don't worry, we'll find it."

When they didn't find the street after a few blocks, Casey got worried that they'd missed it. Then it occurred to him that the whole street was a kind of window, open only for a short time and their one chance was yesterday. Just when Casey was starting to concede that the street was now gone forever, he spotted the familiar old sign hidden by the tree. He stopped his bike. Here it was after all. Duke Street. Neither he nor Arthur said anything.

The others stopped and gathered with them at the mouth of the street. "This it?" Mickey asked.

Casey nodded. "Let's go." Casey entered the street and the rest of the group followed. Kevin and Sean kept close to Mickey, and the three of them looked cautiously in all directions.

"This is pretty scary," Sean said.

"Yeah," Kevin agreed.

"At least it's Sunday afternoon, and not a Monday night."

They toured steadily past the old grocery store and the rundown brick houses, as if it were unwise to go too fast or too slowly. Casey led them to the end of the street, where the little wooden house sat innocently. It was waiting for them, unchanged from the day before.

Casey stared at the fragile structure for a long moment. It was still a bit intimidating. Then he got off his bike. "Come on."

"We really gotta go in there?" Sean protested.

"That's what we came out here for," Mickey said.

"Why don't we wait out here."

Casey turned sharply. "Why, so you can call the cops if something happens?"

"Yeah!"

Casey turned and walked towards the gate.

"You don't need us," Kevin offered weakly.

"Then what'd you come for?" Mickey asked. "I told you on the phone. We don't even know what we're lookin' for. The more help the better." Mickey turned and started to walk up the path. "Do what you want," he added.

The brothers looked at each other. They knew there was no way out of it, and reluctantly followed Mickey towards the old house. "Wait up," Kevin said for no reason.

Casey pulled opened the gate. It stuck for a moment, but he'd expected it to be rusted shut. It even whined only slightly. There were three short front steps and Casey was at the front door. He couldn't see through the window, which was dingy and had an old curtain in back of it. He spotted a doorbell and pushed it. There was no sound and no one came to the door.

"I guess it doesn't work," Mickey decided.

"No one should be living here anyway," Casey said.

"Then why'd you ring?" Kevin asked.

"'Tis just a courtesy," Arthur responded.

"Yeah, now we can just barge in," Mickey announced. "Let's go, Case. Before we get too scared." He put his hand to the front window. "It looks really dark in there."

"Great," Sean said.

Casey glanced at Arthur, then grasped the worn doorknob and turned hard. The door creaked open and rattled on its hinges.

There was an immediate smell of stale air and old furniture. The interior probably got no sunlight and was more like an attic that had been sealed and forgotten.

After a moment, Casey stepped in. The wooden floor let out a sharp creak, as if it hadn't been stepped on in years. Maybe his father had been right about the place collapsing. If he'd been alone Casey might've backed out and gone home. But that was impossible with Arthur and everyone else and all the trouble they'd gone through to get to this point.

"See anything?" Mickey asked behind him.

"Not yet."

"Come on, if you're gonna go in," Kevin said impatiently.

"Relax, I can barely see a foot in front of me." They'd left the front door ajar and only a crack of light entered the cramped room. The windows were black with dirt and covered by dingy old curtains. Casey squinted and inched forward, his eyes still trying to adjust to the darkness.

"Perhaps I should take the initiative," Arthur said and stepped past Casey into the center of the room. He had a sense of the familiar, and realized that the instance reminded him of that first day in Merlin's cottage. The feeling was a mixture of fondness and regret. He wanted desperately to go home and resume his life as it was meant to be. Now that there was real hope, he had no reason to be apprehensive.

"It smells funny in here," Kevin said.

"Yeah," Sean agreed. "Like gran'ma's room."

"Where's the light switch?" Mickey asked.

"This place won't have electricity. I'll open the curtains." Casey stepped towards the window and pulled them back in one swift motion. The light poured in and they could actually see the room for the first time.

"Jeez, what a hole."

"Just start lookin' around," Casey instructed. A few candles sat on the window sill, which struck him as peculiar. The room, a small living room, had an old couch with the stuffing coming out of it. There was also a coffee table, a bureau, a big soft easy chair, and a circular throw rug. The room even had a fireplace and a wooden mantle, on top of which were a few more candles. The room was cluttered with a few old books and magazines, and a lot of old newspapers. But it still looked livable, for upon closer examination, all the furniture was in decent shape and the floor was intact, if a little warped.

"Hey, this place isn't so bad," Mickey

announced. "It looks better than Tony's dorm at school."

"I don't see anything." Casey turned to Arthur. "Arthur?"

"There appears to be nothing of significance," he admitted.

Casey made a sour face and sighed. "It's gotta be here."

"What, Case?" Mickey insisted.

"I don't know, but something." He looked around. "Damn."

"Nothing here in the kitchen," Kevin said, peeking around a flimsy partition. "Unless this old coffee pot means something."

Casey poked his head in and saw the pot sitting atop a small stove. He also spotted a pan, a plate, a glass and a single set of cheap silverware. When he saw the roll of paper towels he got a strange feeling. Casey looked up and spotted the dark entrance to another small room next to the kitchen.

"Hey, what's in here?" Kevin said curiously and stepped into the dark room. An instant later the dead silence was shattered by a loud whack. "Ahh!!!" Kevin screamed. There was another sharp whack. "Ah! Hey, stop!"

"Kev!" Sean cried. "What is it?!"

Everyone rushed to the kitchen, only to be trampled by Kevin as he came flying out of the small room, scared out of his mind.

Casey saw his face, which was virtually unrecognizable with fear. There in the doorway stood an old man, just as frightened, but mad as hell, too.

He was wearing a dirty undershirt and worn out boxer shorts. His eyes were bloodshot and squinting to adjust to the sudden light. Except for the sawed-off broom stick in his hands, he looked like a bear at the mouth of his cave. He'd been startled out of his sleep and he was furious.

"Who're you?!" Casey cried from the throng of confused boys.

"What're you hoodlums doing in my house?!"

"*Your* house?!"

"That's right! I'm Benjamin Duke!"

25

ided by a few prodding blows of his broom stick, the old man threatened the boys until they had retreated to the living room.

But he was ever vigilant, and continued to brandish the weapon aggressively. Every time one of the boys tried to move or speak, Duke screamed at him to get out and banged the stick on the floor in front of him.

"Will you just relax!" Casey protested. "We're not here to steal anything!"

"I ain't got nothin' worth takin' anyways!"

"No kiddin'!" Kevin said.

"Now get outa here afore I call the cops!"

"You don't even have a phone," Casey declared.

"Never you mind about that. Just get goin'." He poked Casey with the broom handle and jumped back nervously.

"Look, we thought no one lived here and we were lookin' for something. We didn't find it so we'll take off. Sorry to bother you."

"Better believe you're going," the old man muttered. "Wake me up without warning like that, scare me half to death." He stepped forward and raised the broom stick like a baseball bat, ready to defend his turf to the end. "Man's home is his castle, you better believe it," he added sourly.

The boys made their way to the door. Arthur hesitated, looking dejected. His eyes darted around the small room one last time.

Duke prodded him with the broom stick. "Let's go, boy. On your way."

"Can I just ask you, sir," Arthur began gingerly, "if there's not something you know... "

The old man banged the stick on the floor in front of him.

"What did I say, boy?! Out, so I can have my tea!"

"Come on Arthur," Casey said. "It's no use." He and the others left quietly, and Arthur turned and followed them out.

Outside, they collected their bikes and got ready to go home. Arthur was slow to join them. He couldn't help but think that there was still something to this old hermit. After looking back once more, he went through the gate and down the path, where the boys were waiting on their bicycles. But at the last moment, he stopped and ran back to the fence, where he stood looking through the dingy front window.

"Arthur?" Casey asked tentatively.

The living room was empty. Then the old man appeared from the kitchen with a steaming metal goblet. A chill went through Arthur's entire body. He suddenly knew what he had to do, as if fate had whispered in his ear. Arthur went back through the gate, up the three small steps, and burst into the old man's house.

The old man was too scared and startled to move. He just cowered in his seat, waiting for Arthur to enact his revenge for being thrown out. His hand shook, and the metal cup looked like it was about to drop from his frail grip.

Outside, the boys ran to the fence to see what was happening. "What's he doing?" Mickey asked. Casey was too stunned to speak. He just hoped that Arthur didn't hurt the old man in his excitement and confusion. He knew that Arthur must be disappointed, but he didn't expect anything like this.

"What... what... " The old man tried to speak but he couldn't get the words out.

"Your tea!" Arthur cried madly. "I must have it!"

"What?"

Arthur had recognized the goblet, which not only looked like the one that the Duke had been drinking from by the fireplace, but which Arthur knew was the very same vessel. It looked as old and used as it was. The old man had to be a descendant of the Duke of Flatbush, and the pewter goblet passed down to him through the centuries. Here it had come to rest, and Arthur knew that he had only to sip from it and he would be transported home.

He took the cup from the old man's withered

hand and raised it to his lips. He tasted the hot, bitter tea, and waited... and waited... and waited, for nothing happened.

When the old man saw the life drain from Arthur's face, he regained his courage and stood up. "Gimme my tea!" he shouted angrily, and snatched the goblet from Arthur's hand with newly found authority. "Now if there's nothing else... " He thumbed Arthur towards the door. Arthur left once again, as the old man grumbled about being attacked during his last and only pleasure in life.

"What was that all about?!" Mickey asked when Arthur joined them and mounted his bicycle.

Arthur shook his head. "I thought sure that..." But he didn't finish the sentence.

Casey could see the sadness in his face. He looked more lost and hopeless than ever. "Arthur, y'all right?" He didn't respond, and appeared to be fighting back tears. "Let us just go home."

They mounted up and started the long ride back. Arthur was last in the procession, and he could barely follow along. He'd been so sure that a drink from the goblet would send him home. Now, for the first time, he doubted that he would ever get back. Arthur had trouble keeping up with Casey and the others, for he couldn't pay much attention to what he was doing. His mind was back in that house, reliving the act of drinking the old man's tea. It should have worked, he thought over and over. It should have worked!

"Come on, Arthur!" Casey called from up ahead. He had stopped and was waiting for Arthur to catch up. It was the third time, and the other guys had lost their patience and decided to keep going. Casey waved, but Arthur didn't respond. Casey wasn't even sure if Arthur had seen him. Casey turned after a moment and rode after the group. But he went slowly enough for Arthur to keep him in sight.

Arthur didn't much care about anything. He could no longer peddle fast enough to keep the bike steady, and after it wobbled and nearly fell over, he just got off and proceeded to walk while holding the bike upright. Casey and the others had pulled away and were nowhere in sight. But Arthur couldn't worry about them or getting lost or even ever getting anywhere again. His plight now seemed truly hopeless, for if his journey back home could not be connected to the Duke's goblet, then Arthur had no other leads or ideas to consider.

He walked slowly but steadily back along Flatbush Avenue, passed through the park again and came out in Grand Army Plaza, at the edge of Casey's neighborhood. Arthur turned left at the nearest street and walked towards 5th Avenue. He was tired and blank and stared at the ground in front of him, as if every step were a chore.

"Arthur?" a soft voice said. When he didn't look up, it spoke again. "Arthur?"

This time he stopped. "Oh, hello Theresa." She was standing in front of him.

"What's wrong?"

"Oh, well, I thought that I could finally go home, but now I don't think I shall ever go back."

She seemed deeply worried by this prediction. Her face took on an expression of concern almost as serious as his. "I don't understand. Why not?"

He realized that she knew little of his predicament concerning the Duke and how he'd sent him there, and explained it to her in detail. Although she did not possess Casey's newly found understanding of Arthur's origins, she listened attentively and appeared to take every word as intended. "So you see," he concluded, "that I am stranded as surely as if I were on an island in the middle of the ocean. Home shall never be mine again."

Theresa was silent for a few minutes, then excitement slowly crept into her face. "No, don't you see? It's not drinking from the cup that's important."

"What?"

"From what you just told me, Arthur, you have to win him over. He must invite you to drink from it."

"Yes, oh yes!" he cried, realizing what he'd missed. "Now I see the sense of it! How could I be so foolish?" He recalled the arrogance and impulsiveness that had resulted in the Duke sending him away in the first place. Now, that same rash behavior at the old man's house had blinded him to the obvious. The Duke had banished him for his conceit, when Arthur had suggested that he be invited to join him for a drink before the fire. Now he'd have to get this last member of the Duke line to do the same. And then a sip from the goblet would surely send him back!

Arthur's face had changed completely. He looked at Theresa and touched her arm. "I'm grateful to you, Theresa. I may never see you again, but I shall never forget you." He kissed her cheek, as if returning hers from the day of the fair. Then Arthur mounted the bike and rode off as fast as he could.

"Arthur?!" Theresa called after him. "Arthur, wait!"

But he didn't slow down and he didn't look back.

26

rthur explained to everyone that he now realized where he'd gone wrong, and that he'd have to win the old man over in order to get home. Casey tried to sound enthusiastic for Arthur's sake, but he wasn't sure just how reliable the theory was, so he was also preparing for the worst. He knew that if this didn't work, Arthur might be too lost to ever figure out the secret of his return. Casey and Mickey asked how they could help, but Arthur claimed that he must do this alone, no matter how long it might take. He explained that it was a test of his will and patience. Obstinacy and impulsiveness had got him into this predicament, and only grace and restraint would get him out. Since the journey had also been a punishment, he fully expected not to be set free until he earned his freedom.

The very next day, while Casey and the others were back in school, Arthur rode all the way out to the small house at the end of Duke Street. He leaned the bike against the inside of the fence and approached the house cautiously. Arthur figured that since it was already afternoon, the old man was probably awake, unlike the day before when all the commotion woke him up. Arthur went up the steps and knocked on the door, loudly but without urgency. He also hoped that the old man was in a better mood than yesterday.

"Mr. Duke!" Arthur called to announce his presence. The less he surprised him the better. "'Tis I, one of the boys from yesterday."

"Huh, what?" came the withered old voice from inside.

Arthur cleared his throat as loudly as he could. "My name is Arthur, and I was here yesterday. Can I see you, please?"

There was no answer, but Arthur heard some grumbling and foot shuffling, which reminded him of Merlin being interrupted in *his* cottage. A few coughs and wheezes near the door told Arthur that the old man was finally on his way. Arthur hoped that he didn't become irate at the very sight of him.

Duke opened the door just a crack. "Yes now, who is it?"

"Arthur, one of the boys from yesterday. I want to apologize for the abrupt intrusion. We didn't know anyone lived here, so we were just as surprised as you." Arthur figured that if the old man knew he was sorry, he'd be less likely to turn him away without hearing him out.

The old man opened the door all the way and Arthur relaxed.

Duke looked him up and down with suspicion. "Mm," he grunted.

"Well, you should be sorry. Lucky I didn't have a heart attack and die on you. Then you'd really have something to be sorry about."

"Yes, sir," Arthur agreed. He steeled himself to be as humble and contrite as he could.

"Well, I'm no worse as you can see, so I guess you can go home satisfied you haven't killed me. Not that it really matters anymore." He started to close the door.

"Wait, sir."

"Why?"

"I really want to make amends. Maybe I could do some work for you."

"Mm, I don't know."

"Isn't there anything you need done? Maybe I can clean your house for you. I feel terrible about yesterday and I'll do anything to make it up to you."

"Why just you? Where are the rest of them?" Duke craned his neck and peered over Arthur's shoulder suspiciously.

"Uh, well... I speak for all of us. We thought if we all showed up you'd get angry again and never even open the door."

"And they were all sorry, too?"

"Yes, but I was the sorriest, so now I'm here." This being humble and gracious really is a test, Arthur thought. It's so much easier being forceful and arrogant. It made him appreciate Merlin's endless prodding and cajoling. If the old man didn't give in now, Arthur didn't know what he'd say next.

Duke's wrinkled, unforgiving face began to slacken. "Hm, maybe. But I don't have much to clean up 'cause I don't have much in the first place."

Arthur nodded towards the dingy living room window. "Your front window needs cleaning, to be sure. I could at least do that."

The old man nodded. "Fair enough," he said firmly. "Come in."

At lunchtime, Theresa spotted Casey and his friends in the cafeteria. She was agitated and ran up to them. "Where's Arthur?" she asked urgently. "He said I may never see him again."

"Don't worry," Casey reassured her.

She told them about meeting Arthur on the way home yesterday, and what he'd told her about the old man on Duke Street. She seemed very concerned, and when she didn't even ask for an explanation of Arthur's true nature, Casey assumed that she somehow understood and accepted it. Casey told her of Arthur's plan to win over the old man, as she herself had suggested, but explained that it would take a while. Theresa then made him promise to inform Arthur of her concern, and Casey assured her that he would be in school later that week and she would see him again anyway.

Theresa left and the gang finished their lunch in silence. They were worried about Arthur, but no one wanted to bring up the subject of his predicament. Success and failure seemed interchangeable. It was as if they all felt the weight of what was happening and were afraid to face it. They knew that when they saw Arthur again, it might well be for the last time.

Arthur was committed to gaining the trust of the old man to the exclusion of all else. That first day, Arthur managed not only to clean Duke's windows, but to get rid of all the old newspapers and other refuse that the old man had got used to ignoring. Duke was a bit nervous at Arthur's enthusiasm, for he thought that the boy seemed unusually determined in his efforts, as if he intended something more than a simple apology. Toward the end of the day, when he told Arthur that he was satisfied with the job and that he could go home, Arthur only seemed interested in finding something else to do for him.

"I'm about ready for my tea," the old man announced, and Arthur realized that he was being told to leave. In the hope of being invited to have some tea, Arthur was tempted to remain. But he forced himself to submit to the labors of the test and decided to say goodbye. He also told Duke that he'd be back tomorrow, and left before the old man could protest.

Arthur returned the next day, and informed Duke that he genuinely wanted to help him in every way. The old man was a little surprised, for despite Arthur's visit the previous day, his presence was still an imposition. Arthur had anticipated this and tried to be friendly. He was determined not to be threatening or manipulative. His intentions had to be sincere for the old man to make a natural journey from being wary to being fully accepting. Indeed, before Arthur's task was through, he would have to make the old man eager to see him, and even ask him to come back again.

As the days went by, Arthur succeeded in cleaning Duke's kitchen and bathroom, buying him food and necessities with money donated by Casey and Mickey, and fixing the rickety steps in front of the house. The old man hovered over Arthur every minute, making crusty remarks designed to maintain his household authority, while sending Arthur the message that even though he was a volunteer, he still had to do a good job.

As he'd hoped, the old man eventually got used to Arthur's presence and began to talk about himself. It had been a long time since he'd had any kind of a real house guest, let alone a regular visitor. By the end of the week, Arthur's main task was to listen to the old man rattle on about the past and seem interested. He told him of how Duke Street had once been a private driveway, owned by his wealthy great grandfather; of his family and its slow deterioration over the years; of his wife and his friends and how they'd moved away or died one by one, until he'd been left alone.

"I had a cat, but she was the last to go. I guess she just crawled off somewhere and died. Just the same, it was getting harder to feed her an' all. F'it wasn't for them social security checks I get at the post office, I'd be eatin' cat food myself. For years I kept expectin' the city to come along and kick me out, tear the whole street down, but when I stopped gettin' rent bills and then even the gas bills stopped comin', I guess they forgot about me altogether. I don't got no 'lectricity, but there's nothin' like free room an' board to stretch the dollar." He laughed a dry, elderly laugh. His existence wasn't much, but at least it was free. This not only made him happy, it made him proud.

"I got my search for old magazines an' yesterday's newspapers, and soda cans an' beer bottles to trade in for a little extra change, so I'm pretty well set. Gets me outa the house, too. Nobody bothers me an' I don't bother them. Can't ask for much more at my age, 'cept a good cup of tea at the end of the day."

"I agree, sir. I got you some real English breakfast tea. It's much stronger than those old bags you were using over and over. It should last you a long while."

He nodded. "Thanks. Guess you know my ways pretty well by now."

"It's been my pleasure getting to know you, Mr. Duke. If there's anything else you need, just tell me and you can consider it done."

"Boy, I'da sweared you were after somethin' when you showed up here again. But since I don't got nothin' you must really be on the level." He looked at the room around him. "This place's never looked better."

"Well, I've never really helped anyone but myself before. But I must if I'm able to go forth and... do what I'm soon meant to do."

"You're a fine boy." The old man leaned forward and patted Arthur on the knee. "Now why don't you join me for a cup of tea before you go."

It had been so unexpected that Arthur could hardly react. "Let me make it for you," he suggested. He got up and went to the kitchen.

"That's fine, my boy."

Arthur heated water on the small gas stove, and opened the tin of tea leaves. Slowly, reverently, he brought out the old pewter cup and held it up. This is it, he thought. Finally, I can now go home. As the water began to boil, it came to him that maybe it had been too easy. Might there be a real test within the test? he asked himself, fearing further mischief by Melora. Did he have the strength to tempt fate? For if Arthur truly had the will and wisdom to be King, he also had the courage to test his right to his destiny.

Arthur made the tea in the old pot and poured it into the gray metal cup. He added a little sugar and then he brought it out to Duke and set it down gingerly before him. It was a ritual presentation.

"Thank you, Arthur. I have only the one cup, but it's good enough for both of us." He held it up proudly. "It's an old family heirloom, in fact."

He forced himself to speak. "Perhaps next time," he said gently. "I have to go now, sir."

The old man seemed disappointed. "Oh, well then, if you come back tomorrow we can share it then. No work, we'll just sit and talk, eh?"

"I'll be here," Arthur said, almost gratefully.

Then he left. Tomorrow's the day, then, he thought. A warm prickly feeling rose in his chest. Arthur needed the extra day, for as desperate as he was to go home, he was still unprepared. There were a few things to be done. He had to see Casey and his friends once more, as well as Cathy and Theresa. And there was one other very important thing to be done before his quest was complete.

Arthur felt good riding back. He was pleased with his calm and his confidence at that crucial moment of the old man's invitation. It would have been so easy to take the tea and just disappear. But he'd displayed the faith and heart to assure himself of his noble place in the world. These qualities were what he'd lacked at the Duke's castle. Arthur could never have imagined them at the time, but he would never be at a loss for them again.

27

n Friday, Arthur showed up at school just as it was letting out. When Casey and Mickey spotted Arthur waiting at the bottom of the steps, they were a bit surprised.

"Still here?" Mickey commented.

"Yes, but not for long I think."

"Really?" Casey asked, searching his face.

Arthur nodded. "I shall be going home tomorrow," he said confidently.

Casey knew he meant it, but he was still preparing for the possibility that Arthur might never leave. He had a hard time imagining it, after all, and part of him just didn't want him to go now. He might've even suggested that he stay, just for a little while longer, but he knew that was impossible, for Arthur belonged elsewhere.

"I wanted to see you all before I left, as well as Cathy and Theresa."

Mickey grinned. "Ah-ha."

Arthur ignored the remark. "I should thank

everyone for all they've done."

"We can always... see you off," Casey ventured.

Arthur shook his head solemnly. "You know I must do this alone."

"Everybody'll be along soon. You can say good-bye and just go back then." Casey didn't want Arthur to leave that day, but he needed to see his reaction to the suggestion.

"I must prepare myself before I go. And it shall be a long walk back to Mr. Duke's. That's why I have to wait until tomorrow."

"What about the bike?" Mickey asked.

"I won't need it anymore."

"Well, at least we have the rest of tonight," Mickey reminded them.

Casey and Arthur stared at each other. It was as if they'd already said their final goodbye.

"Come on," Mickey said. "Let's go to my house."

The next day, Saturday, almost two weeks after Arthur had arrived, he walked to Casey's house with Mickey. The previous night had been tense and subdued. Nobody wanted to talk about Arthur's departure, but nothing they did could hide that it was all they thought about. They went to Kevin and Sean's for a while, then back to Casey's to see Cathy and his parents. They couldn't tell them that Arthur was leaving and they'd never see him again, but Arthur thanked them for being so nice to him. Cathy, whose suspicions had all disappeared, was pricked once again by the peculiarity of the situation. But she couldn't figure out why and said nothing about it. Casey almost wished that she had, for he was compelled to say something about Arthur's identity and what he was preparing to do. He didn't think he'd be able to resist announcing the truth for long, if only to make it more real and inescapable. But since it might result in Arthur's being prevented from going, Casey realized that he could not betray him now and kept quiet.

After Cathy went to the library and Casey's parents left to go shopping, it seemed that they could no longer prolong the inevitable. Arthur solemnly went upstairs to Casey's room, while he and Mickey waited in the kitchen. A short time later, they heard the strange sound of heavy footsteps descending the stairs. There was also the occasional clink of chain mail.

"I'm ready," Arthur announced.

Casey and Mickey went out to the front door, where Arthur stood in full regalia. He looked so different in his tunic and armor, with his sword, now dubbed Excalibur, at his belt. They had seen him like this two weeks ago, and while the costume was the same, it was Arthur himself who had undergone the true change. His face, now confident and sure, had lost its immature arrogance and impatient expectation. His bearing, now strong and stalwart, was free of thoughtless impulse and nervous energy. He had left these adolescent traits behind, and become a king. He even appeared a bit taller and bigger, for he no longer seemed to feel the weight of his armor, nor did Excalibur threaten his footing.

"I guess this is it," Casey said to him. "Next

time we see you, it'll be in the history books."

"'Bye, Arthur," Mickey said. "It's been great. Knowing you and everything."

Arthur smiled a noble, square-jawed smile. "I wish you all could come with me, if only to visit."

Casey and Mickey managed sad smiles.

"One last thing, Casey," Arthur began. "Despite what you told me about witches, I fear Cathy is being enticed into a coven as we speak."

"What makes you say that?"

"After school yesterday, I saw her with a small group of other girls. With my own eyes, I saw fire come from their fingers and smoke from their mouths."

Casey thought for a moment. "There were just smoking cigarettes, Arthur."

"Cigarettes?"

Casey grinned. "It's nothing." He couldn't believe that he was actually going to miss explaining these simple things to Arthur. "Burning leaves. You kinda roll them up and put 'em in your mouth."

"Hm. It sounds quite foul."

"It is, believe me."

"But you're not concerned? I've had extensive dealings with witchery and it's not to be underestimated."

He nodded. "Don't worry. But let's just say, for the sake of argument, that they were a bunch of witches. Wouldn't they at least have the power to keep from getting caught so easily?" Casey waited while Arthur thought for a moment. He wanted to hear him say it just once more.

"Yes, I see the sense of it."

They watched Arthur walk down the front steps and out to the street. He glanced back only once. He moved slowly with his armor on, and it took him a while to disappear down the block and out of sight. But Casey and Mickey could still hear the slight clink of the chain mail, and they listened in silence until they were both sure it had completely faded way.

"I hope he makes it," Casey said eventually.

"Yeah."

Arthur went to Theresa's house before setting out on his last journey to Duke Street. He wanted to see her apart from everyone else, and he wanted her to see him as he now looked. This was the true Arthur, a knight, a warrior, a king, not the lost boy in borrowed clothes. Arthur wanted to see her one last time, so she would remember him in the manner of his real self.

It was less than an hour later that he reached Flatbush Avenue and start walking south. He had to get used to the armor again, for it seemed like ages since he'd last had it on. His pace was slow and steady, like a march. But he felt good, as if he were getting stronger with each step. He'd been in this strange land two long weeks, but he'd grown so much older and wiser. He was ready to go home.

The march through the heart of Brooklyn would take most of the afternoon, but Arthur accepted it as a deserved penance and refused to rush or be impatient. Unlike his trips by bicycle, in the clothes of any teenager, this one resulted in endless stares and comments by curious locals. Arthur was also delayed again and again by demands, questions, and other distractions. But he took them as they came, and didn't evade anyone or anything.

Along the way, Arthur gave the rest of his money to a few poor beggars. He explained who he was to the excited children who gathered around him and followed for a few blocks. He told a group of smirking hooligans why he was dressed so, and even prevented one from robbing an old lady with a flash of his sword. Arthur was then confronted by two policemen on horseback, who noticed the sword on his belt and questioned his identity and intentions. But Arthur was unwavering in his gentle confidence.

"That a real sword, son?"

"Yes sir, and razor sharp it is."

"Just what d'you plan to do with it?"

Arthur could detect a certain belligerence in the officer's tone, but he was determined to ignore it. "Not a thing, unless some blackguard draws his first, I assure you."

The cop grinned. This kid was too serious to take seriously. "I see. You won't be too disappointed if you don't find nobody else with a sword? I mean, you ain't out here just lookin' for trouble, are you?"

Arthur seemed astonished. "You mean actually provoke a confrontation?"

228

He glanced at his partner and grinned, almost laughing. "Yeah, actually that."

"T'would be totally outrageous and against my principles. And thus, against myself, too. I didn't come this far to be thwarted by my own quest for glory."

They nodded and looked him over suspiciously. "Hm. Just where you headed?" the second one asked.

"To the house of the last living descendant of the Duke of Flatbush."

"The Duke of Flatbush?!" the cop repeated incredulously.

"I thought that was Duke Snider," the other said with a burst of laughter.

"Yes, and I shall drink from the Duke's goblet, which has been in his family for a thousand years. Then I shall be sent home to England in my rightful century, where I shall assume my place in history."

"This is just too good to pass up," the cop muttered to his pal. He looked down at Arthur and, as earnestly as possible, asked, "Forgive my ignorance, sir knight, but just who are you?"

"King Arthur."

And then, restraining further laughter, they told Arthur that he could go. "You sure we shouldn't bring him in?" one of them questioned as they rode away.

"It's not worth the paperwork."

"I swear, that's the best get-up I've ever seen."

"Yeah, even the sword looked real."

So Arthur marched on, now halfway to his destination. There were more questions and remarks to be deflected, more curious children eager to touch his armor, and other tempting distractions. Young girls attempted to talk to him and engage his attention. There were even two offers of money if Arthur would allow himself to be employed as a barker. He had but to hand out leaflets, attracting passersby to a huge discount store called King's and a family restaurant known as The Red Carpet, and he'd be twenty dollars richer for the effort. But he politely refused and journeyed on, unfatigued and undeterred.

When the doorbell rang at Casey's house, he was in his room doing his homework. He came downstairs and opened the door. "Theresa?" He couldn't hide his surprise and looked at her as if she were the last person he'd expected to see on his doorstep.

"Where's Arthur?" she asked fearfully.

"He didn't go to your house after he left here? That's what he said—"

She shook her head vigorously. "I wasn't home. I missed him."

"Oh, well he's gone."

"My mother said he was wearing armor and had a sword. She couldn't believe it."

"Yeah, that's what he had on when we found him. He wanted to go back the same way."

"Back! Back where?"

"To... medieval England," Casey said flatly.

"So he's really King Arthur! Are you kidding me?!" Theresa now looked more angry than worried.

Casey was becoming confused. "I thought you knew everything."

"How?! What d'you mean?!" She stared at him as hard as she could.

"You said he told you about the old man and what he had to do to go home."

"I thought that was just part of his, you know, fantasy. What he really meant was that he would somehow be able to go home to his parents if he went through this thing with the tea. It was just a way to... make everything okay in his mind. I was just going along with it. I didn't believe it had anything to do with really being King Arthur. That's crazy."

"Yeah well, he is. What can I tell ya."

"But I have to see him."

"It's probably too late."

"Tell me where he's going and I'll go there."

"It's too far. It's all the way down Flatbush."

"Where? I'm serious. I have to go."

"How?"

"By cab, I have money. Come on, tell me," she pleaded.

"Okay, but I should go with you or you'll never find it."

They left the house and hurried over to Flatbush Avenue to hail a cab. Casey told the driver to go south and he'd tell him where to turn. The Saturday afternoon traffic was unusually light and they cruised along briskly. But Theresa grew increasingly more impatient, as if she expected to arrive at Duke Street after no more than a few blocks. She groaned her frustration as she stared out the cab window, desperately checking each passing street sign.

"Come on, where is it already?" Theresa pleaded. She nervously fingered her gold cross beneath her red scarf, praying that they still had enough time.

Casey said nothing for another ten blocks. Then he blurted out suddenly, "There it is! Okay, next left."

"Thank God."

They turned and the cab slowed to a near stop. As it crept down Duke Street towards the dead end, this part of the trip seemed to take even longer.

"Is that it? Is that the house?!" Theresa cried. She squeezed the door handle, ready to jump out of the cab as soon as it came to a stop.

"Relax. We may be too late," Casey warned.

"We're not, I know it."

Casey told the driver to wait and followed Theresa out the open door. She ran up the walk and went through the gate. When she reached the small porch she stopped at the front door, afraid to go further. She looked back at Casey, who was soon right beside her. They listened for a moment. No sounds came from the inside of the old wooden house. The only thing they could hear was the steady idle of the taxi waiting behind them.

Theresa raised her hand and was about to knock.

"Just go in," Casey demanded. Then he

reached out and took hold of the door knob. In one motion he turned and pushed, and the weak old door flew back.

They stepped in.

"Arthur?" Theresa whimpered.

They were not too late.

She almost shrank from the sight of him. His sword, his bright purple tunic, and his armor, which shone even in the dim light of the small room, defied belief.

Arthur stood in the middle of the room. In his right hand was the old goblet. He saw Theresa's sad, hopeful face and a trace of a smile appeared on his own.

"Wait," she said, and took her red scarf from around her neck and tossed it to him. It sailed through the air and he caught it with his left hand. His fingers squeezed the scarf tightly as he raised the cup to his lips.

When the flash of light had faded and the room was dim once again, Arthur was gone.

"What the hell was that?" the old man cried, squinting and looking around.

28

asey, Mickey, Kevin and Sean were playing football in the park the next day, Sunday. They didn't have the enthusiasm or concentration to play a game, so they resorted to just tossing the ball around. They thought of Arthur and how they would never see him again. Casey was especially distracted. Over the past two weeks he had lived a different life, and now everything was back to normal and he just couldn't adjust. It was two weeks to the day that Arthur had appeared, and it seemed impossible to Casey that his life had changed in such a short time.

The boys shouted occasionally and ran simple fly and slant plays, each taking turns throwing and catching. Casey didn't particularly want to play football, but he also didn't want to do anything else. Being in the park, in virtually the same spot that they'd found Arthur, made Casey feel less hopelessly cut off from him and the whole experience of knowing him. After a while, the routine became distracting, and then mesmerizing, requiring no calls or responses. They ran the plays in silence, as if each of them were alone and the entire exercise a hallucination. It was still early afternoon, and they would have been out there until it got dark, for lack of anything better to do. Then they were interrupted by a strange occurrence. Kevin caught the ball and faded back, while Casey ran straight out and cut over sharply to receive the pass. Kevin cocked his arm and launched the football confidently. It spiraled through the air in a perfect arc, while Casey extended his arms and prepared to catch it. He reached out for the brown ball as it spun right into his hands. Casey squeezed softly, but his palms came together with nothing between them. He thought that he hadn't been paying complete attention and stopped running. Casey looked around, bewildered. But he hadn't missed the ball, for it was nowhere in sight.

"Case?" Kevin called. "What happened?"

"I don't know."

They all convened on the spot and stared at the ground. There was no football, not there or anywhere else as far as they could see. It had simply disappeared in mid-air.

"Maybe we should call the cops," Sean suggested.

29

rthur was unconscious all night and woke up on his own the next day. He knew instantly that he was home. When he came to his senses and his head cleared, Arthur instantly recognized the familiar smell of the forest. That cool, moist, yet pure scent of a world still young. It was nothing like Brooklyn, which had smelled dense and strong, like a big iron pot of smoking refuse that had been on the fire for centuries. Arthur looked down. In his hand was Theresa's red scarf. He put it to his nose, making him recall her dark eyes and raven hair. For a moment he was sad that he would never see her again.

Arthur looked around. He was in the small clearing outside the Duke's black castle. He got up and stared at the great, imposing structure. But he was no longer scared of this part of the forest or the castle, for they were part of his realm, and if all of England were to be united he'd have to appeal to all men everywhere to bring them together.

Arthur resisted the temptation to pound on the castle door to show the Duke that he'd returned at last, in spite of Melora's curse. He fully recalled what an arrogant child he'd been in his presence and did not want to relive the experience. No, he would not entreat the Duke to join him, nor require his nor anyone else's allegiance. Arthur would be a wise and just leader and they would all come to him on their own, to be part of a new era of peace and unity.

Arthur walked back to Merlin's at a leisurely but assured pace. He never felt more confident of his abilities, but he was neither anxious nor too eager over the imminence of his destiny. He was not looking to broadcast his arrival or demonstrate his leadership. He was confident that the right opportunities would come to him in their time.

Not far from Merlin's part of the woods, Arthur encountered a small group of boys. It was his friends. It had been only two weeks since he'd last seen them. But his heart skipped a beat and he flinched, almost stopping. They looked so young and lost and hopeless. Education, Arthur realized, was what they needed, like that of Casey and his friends. A regular hot bath and a toothbrush wouldn't hurt them either.

"Arthur?" one asked, approaching timidly. He barely recognized him now.

"Yes, 'tis I. But not the Arthur you once knew."

"But how—"

Arthur held up his hand. "I must see Merlin,

the old man. He still doesn't know of my return. But we'll all speak again soon."

When he reached the small cottage, Arthur was reassured to see a thin trail of smoke coming from Merlin's chimney. The old man was home. Arthur marched up to the door and knocked with authority. "Merlin? 'Tis I, Arthur."

The door swung open immediately, revealing Merlin's stunned face. He was overjoyed to finally see him again. He was so excited that he hardly noticed Arthur's new demeanor or how much he'd changed. "Arthur! I knew it! I knew I'd found you at last!"

He hurried the boy inside the small room, where he'd spent nearly every day since Arthur's disappearance. "The Duke would offer no help at all, and all Melora did was laugh, the old witch. I've been doing nothing but trying to locate you in the nethervoid of space and time, and when I finally determined where you were, I attempted to summon you back. But the only thing to appear was that strange object there in the corner. I don't even know what it is. Now here you are just the same, so I must've succeeded after all."

Arthur glanced across the room. On the floor sat a brown, egg-shaped ball. "It's a football, Merlin."

"What's a football?"

Arthur grinned and went to pick it up. "It's for a game. You throw it like this." He demonstrated, just as Kevin had showed him that first day in the park, with his fingertips on the laces.

"Why is it called football, if you must use your hands?"

"I still don't know, Merlin. That's something I never found out." Arthur tossed the ball up in the air with casual ease.

Merlin looked at him squarely and saw the new Arthur for the first time. The old man was startled all over again and couldn't speak. "You seem... different, my boy."

The young king couldn't help grinning slightly. "I am."

"You must tell me," Merlin said with anticipation. "You must tell me everything."

"I surely will, Merlin. The future is wondrous."

"But you're happy to be back, no?"

"Oh yes. But... " Arthur looked away and sighed wistfully.

"But what, Arthur?" Merlin pleaded, searching the boy's face with desperate concern.

"How I shall miss spaghetti and meatballs."

Arthur was truly glad to be back where he belonged, with Merlin, at the beginning of a marvelous and unpredictable journey. Now it would commence in earnest, as it was meant to, and he was ready. Arthur removed his chain mail hood and sat down.

He cleared his throat with authority. "Well...," he began, with the manner and diction of one well past his years, and proceeded to tell the first tale in the legend of King Arthur.

About the Author

David M. Korn lives in New York City, where he writes novels, plays and screenplays. He likes dogs, ice cream and is a Yankee fan. Readers can contact him at davidmkorn@earthlink.net.